BERNARD SHAW'S POSTMISTRESS

Jisbella Lyth outside her post office (courtesy David Grapes)

BERNARD SHAW'S POSTMISTRESS

THE MEMOIR OF JISBELLA GEORGINA LYTH AS TOLD TO ROMIE LAMBKIN

Edited by

L.W. Conolly

The Academy of the Shaw Festival

Distributed by Rock's Mills Press

The original edition of this book included the following Library and Archives Canada Cataloguing in Publication information:

Lyth, Jisbella Georgina, -1964, author
    Bernard Shaw's postmistress : the memoir of Jisbella Georgina Lyth as told to Romie Lambkin / edited by L.W. Conolly.

Includes bibliographical references and index.
ISBN 978-1-77506-321-6 (softcover)

    1. Lyth, Jisbella Georgina, -1964. 2. Shaw, Bernard, 1856-1950--Friends and associates. 3. Lyth, Jisbella Georgina, -1964--Travel. 4. Postmasters--England--Ayot St. Lawrence--Biography. I. Lambkin, Romie, author II. Conolly, L. W. (Leonard W.), editor III. Academy of the Shaw Festival (Niagara-on-the-Lake, Ont.), issuing body IV. Title.

PR5366.L98 2019   822'.912   C2018-906515-X

First published in 2018 by
The Academy of the Shaw Festival
P.O. Box 774
Niagara-on-the-Lake, Ontario L0S 1J0
www.shawfest.com

Bernard Shaw's Postmistress is © 2018 Blaise Bullimore. All editorial matter is © 2018 L.W. Conolly.

No part of this publication may be reproduced or stored in a retrieval system, or transmitted in any form or by any means, electronic, mechanical, recording, or otherwise, without written permission of the publisher.

Designed by Aldo Fierro

Cover photo: Jisbella Lyth and Bernard Shaw outside the post office, Ayot St Lawrence.

For Romie and Jisbella

CONTENTS

Acknowledgements • ix

Introduction • 1

Preface, by Romie Lambkin • 7

Note on the Text • 12

Note on British Currency • 12

Bernard Shaw's Postmistress • 15

Notes • 121

Sources Cited • 135

Other Sources Consulted • 135

Index • 137

ACKNOWLEDGEMENTS

I AM INDEBTED TO David Grapes II* for permission to publish the Jisbella Lyth memoir, one of the many gems in his outstanding theatre collection. Blaise Bullimore, son of Romie Lambkin and executor of her estate, has also kindly given his permission. It has not proved possible to trace any surviving relatives of Jisbella Lyth, who died childless. I am immensely grateful to Blaise and his wife Lana for their enthusiastic support of this project from its inception and for providing biographical and other information about Romie Lambkin. Many thanks also to Sue Morgan, Alice McEwan, Philippa Parker, Evelyn Ellis, and Anne Wright for their interest and support. My family publishing team—proofreader Barbara Conolly, copy editor Rebecca Conolly, and designer Aldo Fierro—have again given me the benefit of their formidable skills, and have been discreetly corrective on those (too many) occasions when they have exposed my work, shall we say, as a touch lackadaisical. Friend and fellow Shavian Michel Pharand has also once again hauled me from ignorance to enlightenment in more instances than I care to admit. I also express warm appreciation to Tim Jennings, Executive Director of the Shaw Festival, for his support of this and other Festival publications in which I have been involved.

*Professor of Theater and Founding Director of the School of Theater Arts and Dance at the University of Northern Colorado, where he also serves as the Producing Artistic Director for UNC's professional summer stock company (the Little Theater of the Rockies, founded in 1934), David Grapes has combined a distinguished university teaching and administrative career with award-winning accomplishments as director, actor, drama critic, and playwright. He has provided artistic leadership and has directed and acted at major regional theatres across the United States, is creator or co-creator of several musical reviews and plays that have enjoyed national and international success, and for several years has reviewed plays at Canada's Shaw and Stratford Festivals for the Booth newspaper chain (Michigan), for other media outlets, and for his own online Canadian Theatre Festivals blog. David Grapes began collecting archival theatre materials in 1976, since when he has accumulated a rich research and teaching resource, with particular emphasis on Bernard Shaw and his contemporaries. Holdings in his collection include correspondence, cabinet cards, signed photographs, first editions, programmes, posters, recordings, scripts, ephemera, and memorabilia.

INTRODUCTION

In November 1906 Bernard Shaw and his wife Charlotte acquired a home in the remote village of Ayot St Lawrence in Hertfordshire, about fifty kilometres north of central London. It was a country retreat from their London home, a large flat in fashionable Adelphi Terrace located between the Strand and the (often smelly) River Thames. Although the Shaws later (in 1927) moved their London home to Whitehall Court, a short walk north of the Houses of Parliament, they kept their Ayot home for the rest of their lives. Initially rented, the former rectory (built in 1902 for the local Anglican priest) was purchased by the Shaws in October 1920. After Charlotte's death in September 1943, Shaw lived alone in what was by then widely known as Shaw's Corner until his death in November 1950. A few weeks after Charlotte's death, Shaw offered Shaw's Corner to the National Trust. It was accepted early in 1944, though with some reservations, since Shaw provided no funds for its upkeep after his death. Shaw's Corner is, nonetheless, still (2018) owned and maintained by the National Trust and is open to the public for part of the year (*www.nationaltrust.org.uk/shaws-corner*).

When the Shaws moved to the Ayot rectory, a house they judged to be more utilitarian than in any way aesthetically appealing, Bernard Shaw was far from being the internationally acclaimed playwright and polemicist he had become by the time of his death. But through a series of plays that were produced at London's Court Theatre between 1904 and 1907 (including, for example, *Man and Superman*, *John Bull's Other Island*, *Major Barbara*, *The Doctor's Dilemma*, and *Candida*)—together with an increasing number of productions in Europe and the United States—his playwriting reputation and income were rapidly growing. Much in demand as well as a compelling speaker on political and social issues, Shaw's life was hectic enough by 1906 for a retreat from the maelstrom of activity in London to make good sense. And he and the independently wealthy Charlotte could certainly afford a house with eight bedrooms and two acres of property, for which they quickly employed a housekeeper, a gardener, and two maids—with more staff to come, including a cook and chauffeur (in addition to staff for their London home). Shaw quipped that the inscription on a local gravestone for an Ayot resident who had died in 1895 aged seventy that "Her Time Was Short" was an encouraging sign for the long life he needed in order to accomplish all he had in mind, but it was the tranquillity and isolation of Ayot St Lawrence—where "the last thing of real importance that [had] happened was, perhaps, the Flood"—that appealed. A pub, a small shop, two churches (one in ruins), no public transport, a manor house, and a scattering of mostly Tudor and Elizabethan houses: a "Godforsaken hole," in some respects it might have been (*Postmistress*, p. 51), but it all made for perfect conditions to write, read, and reflect. And if the domestic necessities of the house itself got annoying, Shaw could escape to the small writing hut built for him at the bottom of the long garden—with a rotating mechanism that he could use to catch as much natural light as possible.

It all worked beautifully. The plays, essays, speeches, and honours rolled forth: *Misalliance, Androcles and the Lion, Pygmalion, Common Sense About the War, How to Settle the Irish Question, Heartbreak House, Back to Methuselah, Saint Joan, The Intelligent Woman's Guide to Socialism and Capitalism, The Apple Cart, Village Wooing, On the Rocks, The Political Madhouse in America and Nearer Home, The Millionairess, Everybody's Political What's What?* and much more. The 1925 Nobel Prize for Literature, an Oscar for the screenplay of *Pygmalion* in 1938, Freeman of the City of Dublin in 1946. A knighthood and honorary degrees galore declined. To be sure, not all of his works were written at Shaw's Corner. As a young impecunious writer Shaw had learned to write whenever an opportunity occurred—on buses, on trains, in parks, and, after marriage, now comfortably off, on holidays (insisted upon by Charlotte), in hotels, while visiting friends, and on voyages (also taken at Charlotte's insistence) to all parts of the world. But with few exceptions (the cruises, for example) Shaw was never long away from Ayot St Lawrence and his writing hut. He became a familiar figure in the village: walking, chatting, donating time and money to village causes, even popping into the village pub (though teetotaller and vegetarian Shaw was not there to drink or eat). Shaw and Charlotte spent both world wars in Ayot, safer than central London, though not without its scares and dangers (*Postmistress*, p. 70). And, in the end, it was in Ayot St Lawrence, in the garden of Shaw's Corner, that they decided to have their mingled ashes scattered (*Postmistress*, p. 90).

Shortly after Shaw's death, a Shavian enthusiast named Allan Chappelow had the excellent idea of interviewing village residents about their interaction with and opinions of Shaw. The result, a book called *Shaw the Villager and Human Being* (see Sources Cited, p. 135), recounts the views (mostly, but not always, favourable—Shaw could be brusque and stand-offish) of a wide range of villagers, including the village postmistress, a remarkable woman named Jisbella Lyth.

Jisbella arrived in Ayot St Lawrence in 1930, aged forty-six. She came as the wife of Ambrose Lyth, a retired soldier who had been appointed village postmaster. Six weeks after beginning the job he was dead of a heart attack (*Postmistress*, p. 50), and that might have been the end of Jisbella's life in Ayot St Lawrence had post office officials not had the good sense to appoint her postmistress. Shaw, for one, had good reason to be pleased. For the next twenty years Jisbella Lyth was a constant and reliable presence in charge of a business—postal services—that was essential to Shaw's communication on professional and personal matters with correspondents in the United Kingdom and practically every corner of the world. She was also, to a significant degree, the gatekeeper to Shaw's Corner, the post office often being the first Ayot port of call for visitors with aspirations of meeting or seeing Shaw. The post office was easy to find, but where in the village, many wondered, did Bernard Shaw live, and could Jisbella possibly persuade the great man to spend a few minutes with them? She was sometimes—not always, by any means—able to oblige. And at times of celebration (Shaw's ninetieth birthday, for example) or crisis (his last illness, for example), Jisbella was invariably the first point of contact for the press, many journalists relying on her for breaking news (often offering inducements), and her permission to use the post office telephone to call their editors.

Jisbella Lyth, then, figured prominently in Shaw's life in Ayot St Lawrence in various and helpful ways. Beyond that, however, she made a lasting impact on Shaw's work. Although Shaw never explicitly confirmed it (see his response to Jisbella's direct question, *Postmistress*, p. 67), there is little doubt that Jisbella was the inspiration for the postmistress character (named only as "Z") in his short play *Village Wooing* (written in 1933, first performed in 1934). The connection between the postmistress of Ayot St Lawrence and the postmistress "in a village ... on the Wiltshire downs" was quickly and widely proclaimed, and Jisbella became a celebrity in her own right on occasions when she went to London to see the play (*Postmistress*, p. 108). Articles about her (often with a photograph) appeared in both the local and London press, and she felt proud, she said, to be "immortalized" in the play. Jisbella was also proud of her direct association with Shaw's last completed work, *Bernard Shaw's Rhyming Picture Guide to Ayot Saint*

Lawrence, written by Shaw—and illustrated with his own photographs—after consultation with Jisbella and with exclusive selling rights granted to her (*Postmistress*, p. 78). It is in the *Rhyming Picture Guide* that Shaw's earlier "Godforsaken" description of Ayot St Lawrence is transformed into something approaching affection: "Now let me take you for a walk," he says, "And shew you with a rhyming talk / What our dear village has to shew / And tell you all you need to know."

The *Rhyming Picture Guide* is not mentioned in Allan Chappelow's short interview with Jisbella in *Shaw the Villager and Human Being*, and there is much else about Jisbella's relationship with Shaw that is either not spoken of at all by Chappelow or discussed with Jisbella all too briefly. And had it not been for another newcomer to Ayot—after Shaw's death in this case—the Chappelow interview might have remained the sum total of what we know about Jisbella Lyth. And that would have been a pity.

Enter a young Irish woman named Romie Lambkin. Born in July 1919 in Dover, England, to Irish parents, Romie was raised in towns around Dublin, re-locating as dictated by her father's banking profession. Although a citizen of neutral Ireland, she enlisted during World War II in Britain's Women's Auxiliary Territorial Service, serving in Northern Ireland and Europe as a staff car driver. After the war she worked in Berlin with the Allied Control Commission for Germany, and was still there during the 1948–49 Russian blockade and airlift. On her return to the UK, she married, and subsequently moved to Ayot St Lawrence with her husband (who was working in nearby Luton) and their son on New Year's Eve in 1955. There she met and quickly became close friends with Jisbella Lyth. After just two years in Ayot, however, Romie and her family moved to Yorkshire, where she started a teaching career. After retirement, now widowed, she returned to Ireland, where she ran a bookshop in Howth, on Dublin Bay. She published her wartime memoir, *My Time in The War*, in 1992 and wrote two children's novels, *An Echo of Seals* (1993) and *Japanese Whispers* (1994). She was also a regular broadcaster on Irish radio and a contributor to the *Irish Times* and other newspapers. She died in Dublin in 2001.

Romie Lambkin was aware that Bernard Shaw had lived and died in Ayot St Lawrence, but otherwise had only slender knowledge and appreciation of him and his work. She had grown up in locations with which Dublin-born Shaw would have been familiar, and as a teenager had been impressed enough by *Saint Joan* (the only Shaw play she knew) to choose Joan as her Catholic confirmation saint. But it didn't take Romie long to become fascinated by Jisbella Lyth's accounts of her relationship with Shaw, which, as an aspiring writer, Romie recognized as worth recording. Much to her credit, however, she also recognized the value of Jisbella's own story of her pre-

Ayot life: her underprivileged childhood, rudimentary education, and menial jobs as a young woman; a marriage that both families disapproved of (the wedding was boycotted by all but one family member); her challenging and often dangerous voyage to Hong Kong with Ambrose, her soldier husband; her life with him in Hong Kong; her work-related travels (without her husband) to the United States, Canada, and England; her struggles to find employment in England after the war, particularly as her husband's health deteriorated; the shattering death of Ambrose so soon after he had found the perfect job as Ayot postmaster; and, in later years, her adventures and misadventures as a tourist in Europe.

There was, then, Romie realized, a two-part life story to tell, with Jisbella Lyth at the centre of both. Jisbella considered her celebrity status in Ayot to be merely "reflected glory" from Shaw, and she was never anything but courteous and deferential to him. But the courage, determination, and resourcefulness she showed in her pre-Ayot life continued in the Hertfordshire village that became her home. Despite frequent and debilitating illnesses (she was not expected to survive them on more than one occasion), Jisbella's physical and mental resilience enabled her to establish a thriving, entrepreneurial business in Ayot, from which she derived a significant income from exploiting—with his full knowledge and support—her relationship with Shaw.

All of this Romie Lambkin learned in many formal and informal meetings with Jisbella (and through correspondence after Romie had moved to Yorkshire) until after several months the story—written in the first person—was complete. As Romie explains at the end of the Preface, the typed manuscript ("the precious parcel"), with illustrations, was sent to a publisher. "Will my book be published?" she wonders. "Naturally, I have every hope that it will be but, even if it never is, I have had a wonderful experience and my time has not been wasted, for Jisbella Georgina Lyth has accepted our invitation to come and live with us when she retires." Jisbella, however, never did live with Romie and her family. She died in 1964 and is buried with her husband Ambrose in Ayot St Lawrence, just a short walk from Shaw's Corner and her post office (now [2018] the home of the landlord of the Brocket Arms). However, and albeit some years later than Romie had hoped, her book *has* now been published. Her time was, indeed, not wasted.

Leonard Conolly
Niagara-on-the-Lake, Ontario
December 2018

PREFACE

[*This is a script that Romie Lambkin wrote for broadcast at an undetermined date, but it also serves well as a preface to Jisbella's memoir in that it provides the context in which Romie and Jisbella first met in Ayot St Lawrence, formed a close friendship, and then worked together on the memoir.*]

I HAVE JUST FINISHED writing the life story of an elderly postmistress. "Oh, how *dull*" is what you are thinking, isn't it? But don't switch off yet; *my* postmistress is rather a special one. There is nothing dull about Jisbella Georgina Lyth, not even her name. Her tiny sub post office in the Hertfordshire village of Ayot St. Lawrence is known throughout the world, because of the association with George Bernard Shaw, who was Jisbella's friend and neighbour for over twenty years.

Quite apart from this, her own life and adventures in China, Japan, and America would fill a book worth reading. But I'm not going to tell you what I have already written, and which I hope will be published, because then you mightn't buy a copy of my book at all and that wouldn't do my royalties any good. What I am going to tell you is how it came about that I was chosen to write Jisbella's story, and of the fun, hard work, and various tribulations that went into getting it written.

Due to my husband's change of employment we needed a roof over our heads within reasonable distance of Luton. We were fortunate in having friends already living in Ayot St. Lawrence, and when they wrote to say there was a vacant cottage in the village we set off hot foot to look it over.

Knowing that G.B.S. had lived and died in little Ayot and that his house was now owned by the National Trust and open to the public, I felt vaguely pleased at the prospect of actually living in such a famous spot. On that short visit of inspection my feelings swayed between delight at the old world charm of this hamlet, and slight misgivings at its complete isolation. Although only twenty-five odd miles from London as the crow flies, unless you owned a car Ayot St. Lawrence was extremely difficult to get to. There were no buses and the nearest station was two and a half miles away, and that wasn't on the main line either. There were no shops in the village although there was a charming and ancient inn and, of course, the Tudor cottage post office.

The little cottage we came to see didn't strike us too favourably at first. Admittedly it was the middle of winter and the cottage was empty but for a carpeting of dead leaves on the floors, but the dark green of the kitchen, and the fact that an old ruined church and cemetery adjoined it, depressed me more than a little. We departed, thought hard for several days, and decided to take it provided the interior was re-decorated throughout, all paintwork to be white.

On the last day of December 1955, a wickedly cold day, we got ourselves, excited small son, pet rabbit, and furniture out of the removal van and into our new abode. Everything was sparkling, the kitchen positively dazzling under its coating of clinically white paint. A bright fire soon stopped our chattering teeth and hot coffee was waiting for us to drink. Our friends had organized everything for us—coal, bread, and milk—they were all there. By night time we were cosy and snug, and we had time to pause for reflection. If I don't write here I never will, I thought, listening to the utter silence of the night, broken only by a hooting owl and a distant dog barking.

No entertainment could be expected beyond a visit to the inn, a mere fifty yards from our door by the way, but when I sauntered along with my husband for an evening restorative, more often than not we were the only customers, which was not very exciting. We are not TV fans and had no television set. In fact we hadn't even a radio at that time due to a certain disagreement between my husband and myself on the matter. He is a background listener and I am not, so we were trying life without one. Neither did we have a car, although we hastened to acquire an old jalopy as it was a sheer necessity if I was ever to see civilization.

"Yes, I shall certainly *have* to do some writing here," I told myself wryly, and even went so far as to draft a few articles. This wanting to write has been a hobby with me for as long as I can remember, and some of my small efforts did get published, but I suffer from an inability to persevere. There is always something I have to do first, a book I must read, a letter to write, or else I am too tired. A case of tomorrow, always tomorrow. I must feel strongly about a subject if I am to write about it successfully. "But here," I continued my soliloquy hopefully, "I have absolutely no excuse. There's nothing else to do. The surroundings and atmosphere of Ayot *should* inspire me, and also the fact that G.B.S. picked on this village as the perfect place for writing his plays."

Not that I expected to emulate Mr. Shaw. So I did try a little but only scored an occasional bull's eye. One of these articles was an account of my visit to a local dogs' home, where I fell in love with a sad-eyed Collie dog, took her home, made a great fuss of her, and called her Sherry. It appeared in the county magazine under my maiden name, which I always use when I write. [Romie's married name was Bullimore.] Two and two were put together in the village and, finally, postmistress Jisbella taxed me with it. Quite true, I confessed.

By this time I knew Jisbella well enough to spend a little while chatting each time I called to her post office, which was indeed almost every day, although not so much for stamps, as you might suppose, but to see if she had any shillings for my ravenously hungry electric meter [see note 180, p. 134]. We had progressed from remarks about the weather to more personal topics, and I began to hear a little about George Bernard Shaw the man, an erstwhile resident of Ayot. Now I had never been particularly interested in Shaw and had read little of his works but, as I listened to Jisbella's anecdotes, I began to like what I heard of him. So vivid were her word pictures that I half expected to meet the thin, white-bearded figure striding through the village lanes when I was out walking with Blaise, my little boy, and Sherry. She loaned me magazines and books in which G.B.S., Ayot, and herself were pictured and described. These ranged from the American *Life* and *Time* to obscure Indian journals. "My you are famous!" I would exclaim but she called it reflected glory. She had broadcast and appeared on TV in connection with her friendship with G.B.S. Her little living room was almost a Shaw room in itself. On every wall hung framed photographs of Shaw, Mrs. Shaw, his house, and Ayot, all given to her by him. I had heard that Jisbella was the original character on whom Shaw based his one act play *Village Wooing*. Was it true, I asked her? It was.

At this point I thought how much I should like to write her story, but I felt far too inadequate a writer to say so to her. It came as quite a surprise to me to hear her talk knowledgeably of Hong Kong, New York, Vancouver, and Tokyo. She had been to them all, which just goes to show that one should never take for granted that an elderly, silver-haired little lady of seventy-four has never been young, as one is so often apt to do unfortunately. But even at seventy-four, Jisbella wasn't old except in years. Her mind was as sharp as a razor, and her tongue swift with witty remarks or slightly caustic repartee. For a long time I wanted to ask her to join us at the inn next door for a drink, but I was afraid to do so in case she didn't approve of such goings on. I needn't have worried. She blew in one evening with some friends, and I was both amazed and delighted to accept her invitation to "have a Guinness with me."

After that she often joined us, and came to our house for a meal and a chat but, although she often told me she liked my style of writing, I never received the invitation I longed for, to write her life story. It wasn't until she knew that our days in Ayot were numbered, yes my husband was moving again, that she announced, "Oh, dear! I was hoping you'd write my life story for me but I've been afraid to ask you."

"Better late than never," I gasped ungraciously and so, between laughing at our foolishness, we agreed to start at once.

We had almost two months as it turned out as my husband was having difficulty in finding accommodation for us up North as, having sampled the lovely peaceful life in Ayot, I was hard to please. So, without a husband, I was able to devote my entire evenings to postmistress Jisbella, or what was left of them by the time Blaise stopped yelling down the stairs and went to sleep. He was missing Daddy rather badly. By then both Jisbella and I were tired, she from a day's work at her age, and me from a child's demands at my age—thirty-eight if you must know! There we sat, me with pencil and notebook at the ready, shooting question after question at my old friend, stopping her here as she got off the subject, starting her somewhere else, jogging her memory at every turn. Poor woman, an hour or so of this was quite enough to exhaust her, and we both grew a little irritable until we relaxed over a Guinness nightcap.

We gave ourselves Saturday nights off to meet friends at the local, and either played a game of dominoes or just talked. It was usually then that she would recount, quite casually, some wonderful material for our book. We had decided to keep the endeavour entirely secret having no wish to make fools of ourselves should it come to nothing, so I started to carry pencil and paper with me and hurriedly wrote surreptitious notes in case these gems of information be forgotten. Again, Jisbella would remember something vital in the middle of the night, and she had to keep pencil and paper handy to scribble it down. In the morning, like as not, she couldn't decipher it and gave it to me to work out. I had bits of paper here and bits of paper there, all to be enlarged upon and included in my notebooks which were swelling rapidly in a highly confusing way. Although we intended to deal with things as they happened to her, it didn't work out like that. The miscellaneous bits that popped up in her mind had to be noted at once or they might be lost forever. Consequently my notebooks became more of a jigsaw puzzle daily.

In the middle of these dragging and pumping operations, poor Jisbella collapsed into bed with the most terrifying nosebleeds, and she was removed to hospital for over a week. Sherry, my dog, chose the same time to produce nine puppies, changing in the process from the most docile and sweet-tempered animal to a ferociously protective mother. She would have no one in the house except Blaise and myself, and even we had to steer clear of the whelping box. She allowed me to feed her but I could only change her bedding when nature insisted that she went outside for a few minutes. For their own safety, I had to keep all doors locked against my son's playmates who were, of course, just dying to see the puppies. Thank Heaven, Sherry became more amenable after the first ten days and when Jisbella returned home, looking awful, she was the first person allowed to enter the house and view the litter. And so we began work again but at a less exacting pace, and when it was time for me to spring clean, sort out, and pack up prior to moving house, I had all the information I needed, *somewhere*!

The upheaval, and parting from Jisbella and by now dearly loved little Ayot, the actual removal of furnishings plus Sherry and her puppies, and the necessary settling-in activities in Yorkshire took its toll of my time and energy. For some six weeks my duties consisted of feeding puppies, retrieving them from the next door garden every fifteen minutes, cleaning up after them, and exercising Sherry, combined with the usual housewifery of home and child care. When, at last, the last pup was sold I got out my typewriter and started to sort Jisbella's life into some sort of chronological order, not to mention the letters she wrote me almost daily with new bits she'd remembered in the small hours of the morning. I was lucky to find a little nursery locally where, after much coaxing, cajolery, and perseverance, I managed to persuade Blaise to visit each afternoon. This gave me two-and-a-half hours to myself and, with luck and if I wasn't flat out, another two at night, and so the struggle went on.

The first rough draft was, miraculously, finished although it never would have been except that I had promised to write this book, and a promise is a promise. With this draft in our hold-all, my husband having a week's holiday, we returned to Ayot for a blissful stay in Jisbella's lovely old cottage. There were many distractions from children, and reunion celebrations with friends, but we managed to run through the rough copy correcting, inserting, and striking out where needed. Back we went to Yorkshire while Jisbella set off for her autumnal holiday to Monte Carlo, the object being to absorb enough sun to see her safely through the winter. The moment she stepped off the plane on her return to this country she collapsed again. It was a good ten days before I could locate her for she was too ill to write and, for the next six weeks, I was very anxious about her as she lay in hospital. I worked on, hoping to finish the book in time for Christmas. With a great effort I did so and, best of all, my favourite postmistress struggled all the way here to convalesce with us for the festive season, the completed ms. being her Christmas present from me.

The work was done, but even then there were difficulties. Photographs had to be taken of various documents for illustrations, and permission to be sought to reproduce pictures we already had and, oh dear, didn't they know how to charge. But, at last, everything was ready and off went the precious parcel. Will my book be published? Naturally, I have every hope that it will be but, even if it never is, I have had a wonderful experience and my time has not been wasted, for Jisbella Georgina Lyth has accepted our invitation to come and live with us when she retires.

NOTE ON THE TEXT

The surviving text of Jisbella Lyth's memoir is a typescript, now in the David Grapes II Theatre Collection, consisting mostly of carbon copies, so probably not the one (now lost) that Romie Lambkin refers to at the end of the Preface as having been sent to a publisher (unnamed). The typescript is untitled; the title and subtitle used for this book have been created by the editor. One or two pages are missing from the typescript (see below, p. 21), and there is a fragment that doesn't have an obvious place in the surviving text. The fragment reads, intriguingly, "happened to the venison, we certainly never ate it. I suspect it had a midnight burial. The horrible event turned me against blood sports forever and ever." Whatever the circumstances of the incident, Jisbella's resolution would certainly have pleased Shaw. For the most part, the typescript is perfectly legible, though occasional smudges create transcription challenges. Any editorial conjectures are enclosed in square brackets, as are words that have been inserted to fill obvious gaps or to help clarify meaning. Such instances, however, are infrequent. Obvious typographical errors have been silently corrected, and inconsistent punctuation, verb tenses, and capitalization have been standardized. All underlined words and phrases in the typescript have been italicized, as have titles of books, plays, newspapers, and magazines. Spellings of place names have also been standardized (e.g., Milwauki/Milwaukee). There are occasional handwritten corrections—by Romie Lambkin—in the typescript; these have been incorporated into the text. While varying occasionally in detail, the text of the memoir published here is entirely faithful to the original.

NOTE ON BRITISH CURRENCY

Prior to decimalization in 1971, which divided the pound into one hundred pence, British currency consisted of three basic units: pounds, shillings, and pence. There were twenty shillings to a pound, and twelve pence to a shilling. The notation for the pound was (and remains) "£"; the notations for shillings and pence were "s." and "d.". Thus three pounds, three shillings, and three pence is stated £3.3s.3d. The shillings notation might also appear as "/-"; thus three shillings is 3/-. A crown (rarely used) was five shillings; half-a-crown (more common) was two shillings and six pence. A guinea was twenty-one shillings.

Romie Lambkin and Jisbella Lyth at the Ayot St Lawrence Post Office

Romie Lambkin and Jisbella Lyth working on the memoir outside the Ayot St Lawrence Post Office (courtesy Blaise Bullimore)

BERNARD SHAW'S POSTMISTRESS

The Memoir of Jisbella Georgina Lyth

Chapter 1

When I was first approached for my life story, some years ago,[1] I wilted under the barrage of questions fired at me by the writer and soon gave up. "Go back further," he would say, and I would start again. "No, further. Go back further in your life." All I could say to this was that if I went any further back he would have me in my mother's womb. I did not feel well enough to cope with him then but now that I am seventy-four, and [with] gentle prods from my biographer, I intend to enjoy the telling of my story. This time though my starting point will be when I was ten years old.

That was the year I became Stop Press news in the local newspaper. "A Timely Rescue" they called it. I had fallen down the family well and if I hadn't managed to shout for Snowdrop, my sister, as I tumbled in it might have been the last time I saw my name in print. Snow wasn't around anyway but mother, snatching a few minutes upstairs to change her dress, heard the urgency in my cry and dropped everything to charge outside. Fortunately for her she was still fully clothed. In the yard, she found Frisk, our blind spaniel, madly running round and round the top of the well. Sure now of what she feared, she looked down the well to see my long chestnut locks floating on top of the water. By then I was unconscious, having knocked my head on the way down. Poor mother. She felt her legs taking long, slow motion strides to the cottage next door where the village policeman lived. My luck was in for there he was, off duty.

"Jisbella..." gasped mother, "... in the well..."

He took one look at her face and leaped to his feet, snatching up a shepherd's crook he kept in the kitchen corner.

"Quick," he yelled. "Run, Run."

In seconds, he had started fishing for me with his crook, hooking my hair first, [though] he couldn't do much with that. In the end, he slipped it beneath my armpit and started hauling with mother's frantic assistance which hindered more than helped the poor man. As soon as he landed me like a dying fish he applied artificial respiration to get me breathing, although I would almost rather he hadn't I felt so ill, but by the time I'd been stripped and wrapped up in the blankets my panting mother had fetched I began to feel better. At this stage she, too, recovered enough to demand an explanation as to how I came to be in the well at all, it being strictly out of bounds to us youngsters when no grown ups were around. I explained that I was drawing water for the tea thinking I'd save her the job. She always insisted on freshly-drawn well water to boil for our tea. She was so touched by the explanation she carried me up to bed without scolding me at all.

When father came home my brothers and sisters gave him a secondhand, slightly coloured, version of the affair. It did not appear to spoil his appetite for tea that he had almost lost one of his brood. But father wasn't as hard as he sometimes tried to make out. When he had eaten his fill, he came upstairs to joke and kiss me, saying "Why didn't you bring up those buckets from the well, girl?" and departed downstairs again to ferret out his cherished water divining hazel twig to locate another spring in the lawn. His new well ended up with a circumference so small that even Frisk would have a job falling down it, so small it was difficult to get the bucket up and down, as mother pointed out, but it was safe. He filled the old well in and covered it over, so that was that, except for the teasing I had to put up with at school from friends thrilled with the newspaper article featuring Jisbella Georgina.

The cottage we lived in was picturesque, thatched and half-timbered, in the Hampshire village of Brockenhurst,[2] on the fringe of the New Forest. It was thatched so heavily the roof at the back of the cottage was only a few feet from the ground. Some photographers visiting the village asked father to pose in his garden for them one day, which he did in the act of wielding his spade. Months later we were astonished to receive a parcel with this photograph pasted on top, the inscription beneath saying: "To the Tenant of this cottage, Brockenhurst, Hampshire." Unable to recall father's name, the photographer hit on this method to send us a dozen copies of his picture.

Father was a smallholder and market gardener. Forest Rights went with our cottage which meant our livestock could graze at will there and, another valuable asset, he could cut as much peat as we needed for our winter fuel. He used the traditional half-crescent spade for this, we children rolling it up and packing it into panniers on the donkey's back until they would hold no more. We considered ourselves rich having something of every description, pony and trap, mule, donkey, geese, ducks, and chickens. I was my father's poultry maid, gathering the eggs and keeping records of the hens' sittings. When we came home from school our first chore was to fetch the cattle in for milking. In those days, they wore bells to make it easier for us to find them, knowing they were ours not another's because no farmer's bell tinkled alike. The six of us had plenty to do, weeding to do in the garden, fruit to pick, the cart to get ready for the men to take to market. We roamed the forest, too. The countryside close by was more moorland than forest with flaring bushes of gorse or masses of purple heather in their seasons, but many is the mile our young legs covered exploring woodlands and moors in search of blackberries, crab apples, bilberries, and mushrooms. Mother made jellies and preserves until the store cupboards overflowed with goodness. Our surplus pickings went to the market to swell the family budget.

Our baker's oven had its own outhouse. The bundles of faggots we collected heated it and when it was hot enough, which needed mother's expert eye to judge, she raked out the fire and pushed in the bread dough on her long baker's shovel. When the bread turned to a crusty, mouthwatering golden brown, the cakes took their turn. When the baking was finished you would think it should feed an army but it only kept us going for a week.

Nothing was wasted, not even the old golf balls my brother Douglas brought home—he worked as a caddy on the local golf course—father melted them down to gutta percha[3] which he used to repair our shoes, a good cobbler he was, too. My brother proved to be such a naturally good golfer that the club's professional golfer, who lodged with us, wanted father to apprentice the lad to him. The apprenticeship fees were [beyond] our means but the professional was determined; he mentioned my brother to the local JP who was so impressed he did the paying. Douglas's success repaid him.

Chapter 2

When I was fourteen and about to embark upon my very first job as a kennel maid my mother sent me off with this advice in my wicker dress basket:

> Don't go to the theatre, lecture, or Ball
> But stay in your room tonight.
> Deny yourself to the friends that call
> And a good long letter write.
> Don't think that the young and giddy friends,
> That make your pastimes gay,
> Have half the anxious thoughts of you
> That the old folk have today.
> Write to the dear old folks at home
> With locks fast turning grey
> Lest their thoughts go wandering back
> To many a bygone night...[4]

There is a lot more in the same vein but mercifully I've forgotten it. Anyway, I didn't have any social engagements to prevent me writing home as she feared. The ten pounds a year wage agreed to between my parents and the lady breeder sounded a fortune to me. Even though the kennels were not far off in miles I had to live in and that didn't suit me at all; I was terribly, abysmally homesick and, in those times, serving wenches and the like did not see home for months at a time. My misery was so obvious the lady eventually called me to her room to ask what was wrong.

"Don't know," I gulped.

"Would you like to go home?" she asked, with some perception.

"Yes," I wailed in a waterfall of tears.

Father was sent for. "What has been done to my child?" cried my mother as soon as she beheld me. As nothing had been done to me, a few days' holiday and commonsense talking sent me back to work. The homesickness died down bit by bit. As I was passionately fond of animals, I settled down to grooming, feeding, and exercising the pointed-nose fox terriers for my employer to show at Earl's Court.[5] I became a dab hand at picking out future prizewinners from a litter of pups. But after three years I wanted to earn a bit more and decided to move myself into the kitchens of a large house to learn how to cook for the gentry.

A long time went by before I was allowed to cook anything; kitchen maids had more to do than that, like getting up at six-thirty each morning to light the fires and heat the water for the family's ablutions and then, once a week, it was five-thirty rise to clean out the flues of the huge coal range, a job that was essential if the thing was to function efficiently. The rest of my time was spent running around on general messages and fetching, carrying, and preparing Cook's ingredients. For these labours I was paid an annual £16 and out of that I had to buy my own aprons, caps, and print dress. Cook demanded everything be at hand the exact moment required in tune with her tips on how I should *not* do this and that. She was a Yorkshire woman, kind but strict, but she became fond of me because I was what she called droll, not that I quite knew what she meant, but now and then she told me I was the best little kitchen maid she ever had and she'd had a few in her time. Mistress of all she surveyed, she'd send me to bed early, call me in the morning, and see that I ate nourishing foods. I was more than ready for my little truckle bed[6] when nine o'clock struck. Sunday morning one week and Sunday afternoon the next were free.

We underlings had no bathroom. We bathed in a portable zinc model which was issued to us by rotation and carted upstairs to our rooms in the attic, filled with buckets of hot water dragged up from the kitchen. Although I was happy I did wonder what else life could offer me so, by the time I was twenty and no longer an apprentice, I took my first job, junior cook in a Bournemouth school, and almost burned the place down during my first Christmas staff party there, to which I had been allowed to invite my parents and sister Poppy, who wanted to see my presents. I dashed up to my room, taper in hand, unwrapped the tissue-wrapped gifts in my wicker dress basket and ran down to show them off. Then my sister wanted to see Tim, her little cat—I was looking after him for some reason I don't remember—obligingly, I again ran upstairs to fetch him. I smelled smoke halfway.

The smell grew stronger and stronger. I opened the door of my room. "FIRE! FIRE!" I screamed at the top of my voice. Father was first off the mark. He snatched a towel from a bathroom on the way up to beat his way through the dense smoke to find the remains of my dress basket about to burst into full flame. It was pure luck that I had closed the window against the cold instead of airing the room nonstop as was my wont. Tim, the puss, did not turn up until next day so I was the only one to suffer any consequences. My popularity waned considerably.

A domestic servant, I began to realise, didn't need much intelligence to be a success. I once told my mistress this but she did not understand what I meant. That left me feeling I surpassed her in [...]

[*At this point in the manuscript a page is missing. It seems to have introduced Jim—another domestic servant—and Ambrose into the narrative.*]

After this, Ambrose and Jim often went out together, Ambrose talking to me in a friendly way when he called to the house but showing no signs of inviting me out. Jim guessed I wouldn't object if he did, teasing me until I tossed my head scornfully, implying "A soldier? Never." When he dared Ambrose to write me a note suggesting a meeting on my day off, he did not tell me a thing about it. The letter set out a time and date on a busy street corner which happened to exactly coincide with the arrangement I already had with another admirer. The dilemma was great. I asked my friend the parlour maid what she would do if she was me. "Go [to] the one you like best," she said, so I did, but I felt mean disguising myself in a large hat and flowing veil so that my first suitor wouldn't give me another glance. A lifetime of Jiz and Am began that evening.

Am was thirty-two then, fair and well built with blue eyes and artistic hands. He wore a faint moustache which I thought charming but his friends called it an "eleven a side" one.[7] He was a steady fellow, conscientious and teetotal, even going so far as to preach against the evils of drink on occasions. But he was no killjoy, far from it, he was the life and soul of any party we ever went to. Music was his love. He longed to play the piano but a childhood fall left him with a permanently stiffened left hand, not bad enough for the army to turn him down as a clerk, but not flexible enough for the piano. His tenor voice compensated him—he had just passed a voice test for the Carl Rosa Opera company[8]—but the uncle he lived with thought little of professional singers, a more secure life for Am would be to work his way up in the same string of drapery stores where he was manager. Poor Am went through hell in those early [years], it being the usual run of apprenticeship for the boys to be told to dust the eyes of needles, measure the cotton on a reel, or go to a nearby draper for a stand which, of course, they got, the poor ninnies faithfully carrying such orders until a more merciful soul let them off the hooks. He stuck the job for eleven years, the uncle continuing to treat him as a raw recruit until, suddenly, Am rebelled and enlisted in the army. In three months he was in Africa taking a mild part in the Boer War.[9] He was there five years and loved every minute before coming back to base to meet me.

Almost all our courtship was conducted on wheels, both of us mad on cycling, and secluded spots were easier to reach that way. That's how it went for the next eighteen months. Although I was enjoying myself I bore the trombone player[10] in mind and determined not to get too involved. Then the blackmail began. Am volunteered for further African service but, he said, slyly, it was up to me, if I liked him enough he could withdraw his application. I gathered what he was hinting at and dithered about what to do before, at last, admitting to him and myself I'd rather he decided to stay where I could keep my eye on him. I was thinking particularly of the way he talked about teaching English to the daughter of a Norwegian family he knew in Africa, whose dancing he always praised to the skies. The only dancing I was good at was the polka so I was not keen for him to meet her again. I gave in, gracefully, and became engaged.

The idea was not popular with his folks or with mine. Am was a Roman Catholic, although not a particularly devout one that I could see, *and* a soldier, a combination that filled my parents with apprehension. One of my sisters wrote me an angry letter to say that all soldiers thought about was making babies. As it turned out, I had no baby at all but my three sisters had thirteen between them. Am's relations were horrified because I *wasn't* a Roman Catholic. Well, we carried on despite all the opposition and scouted around for a house near Ash, in Surrey,[11] where Am was stationed. We found a six-roomed villa house with windows gazing on to a wide open common in front. The rent was six shillings a week. From this new home, we sallied forth on our own to get married in the village church without the blessing of the Roman Catholic church. The only one from either family [to attend] was Snowdrop, my sister.

Staunch teetotallers or not, we had a wonderful celebration party surrounded by a score of Am's theatrical friends. Long afterwards, Snowdrop told me she had a bottle of port hidden in her bed to make the party even livelier as soon as Am and I set off to cycle the fifty miles to Princes Risborough for our honeymoon.[12]

After the honeymoon, I took in a paying guest, his twenty-five shillings a week helping us to furnish the house more luxuriously. One morning, a lady on horseback whistled me out to her. "Your landlord says you are a professional cook," she said. "Can you come and help me out—my French cook has let me down." As she only lived across the common I gave it a try. Once she had sampled my cooking she would not let me go, even paying a woman to clean my house and arranged for both Am and my paying guest to eat at her house too. That is how the next four years went, happy years they were except we would have liked a baby to come along. By then, too, our families had forgotten to ostracise us, all forgiven and forgotten, my Am choice even admired by my mother and father, and who wouldn't, thought I, Am the best in the world, and a gentleman to boot.

But I found that nothing can be relied on to remain unchanged when you are a soldier's wife when Am came home in a fit of excitement one evening.

"How would you like to go to Hong Kong?" said he, smiling all over his face.

"China!" I gasped, my acquaintance to that country limited to one visit to a Chinese laundry with Am's shirt collars. Beautifully done, they were, too. I pictured myself somewhere very steamy and hot and surrounded by small yellow men and women wearing long pigtails and perennially engaged in washing clothes. Luckily, Am was more enlightened. Hong Kong is very civilized, he said. I went to the library to study every book dealing with Hong Kong, confusing myself a good deal, but one thing I was sure of and that was, once the initial shock wore off, I was raring to go. "Can you imagine me, Jisbella, in China?" I wrote to my family. Naturally, they couldn't.

The whole procedure was thrillingly unusual for me, buying tropical clothes, getting passports, storing our household goods, inoculations, farewell journey home to Brockenhurst. Mother did not seem well and this worried me so much that I went to her doctor and he assured me she was just very tired. Had I thought there was more to it than that I would have let Am carry on alone. We embarked on the Japan and China bound P&O boat, SS *Borneo*,[13] on the first of November, 1913, me with a scared and sinking feeling. Am was infuriatingly blasé. We travelled second class, the height of luxury to me, the only snag a lack of cabin accommodation for married couples, so I shared mine with two other ladies in a similar plight, or in the ship's hospital being dosed with evil-looking black pills when the Bay of Biscay discovered me to be no rough weather sailor. I saw little of Am. Just the same, I knew I was lucky not to be on a troopship for I'd heard tales of soldiers and their wives being packed on board them like sardines. If Am hadn't been a single replacement of office staff it would have been my fate. We ran into a ferocious storm near Colombo. "It's all right, ladies," the steward shouted when he saw us huddle together in fright, "the ship will turn over twice before she goes down."

That might have cheered some hardier women than me. I would have preferred the ship to sink and put me out of my seasick misery. When we docked safely at Colombo Am thought a trip ashore would raise my morale.

As I could hardly wait to reach dry land, I agreed eagerly, and promptly fainted the second I put my foot to the ground and had to be ignominiously carried back on board. By Singapore I had improved enough to spend a few hours shopping. By Kuala Lumpur I lunched ashore and, in Penang, I went to the pictures. That was all I saw of the world in that six-and-a-half-week sea trip; I might as well have stayed at home. But Am had a marvellous time organising and singing in ship concerts, playing deck games and acquiring a beautiful tan in spite of his fair skin. The only morning I was able to face a breakfast was the one we docked in Hong Kong. Determined to make up for lost time, I was working my way through the porridge, kippers, chops, steaks, and soda scones when the cable advising me of my mother's death was brought to the table.

Chapter 3

This Missee's next jump off was to the United States of America![14] Yes, the work of the Walkers again, bless them. They decided it was high time young Jack and Dick did some real schooling and, as Hong Kong had none suitable to offer them, it entailed their going to a boarding school in the U.S. When it was mooted that I, too, should go along to help Mrs. Walker out on the trip, and until the boys got fixed up, I was highly delighted. There was an added inducement that made me jump at the chance with even greater enthusiasm; Mr. Walker offered to pay my fare from New York to England for a holiday, the idea being I could then return to Hong Kong direct from there. Yes, please, I thought and ran home at the rate of knots to ask Am if he would mind terribly. He did mind, of course, but thought it was too good an opportunity for me to miss, knowing full well I would not see home again in the normal course of events until his term of duty was up, whenever that might be, but neither of us had any idea thirteen months would pass before we were together again. (That visit home to England never did come off, by the way, but it was no fault of Mr. Walker's; it was entirely due to the entry of America into the war during our stay in the States.)

I must have been getting used to ocean voyages by this time for the twenty-day trip across the Pacific on the *Empress of Asia* passed off very smoothly with me on my feet all the way.[15] We called at Yokohama so, once more, I was able to enjoy the heavenly Inland Sea of Japan; and at Manila we stopped long enough to hire a carriage for a ride along the Luneta, the fashionable sea promenade, but oh, it was hot. The boys begged for a swim to which request we not only agreed but were only too happy to join them in the water in a vain attempt to cool off.

I did not envy Mrs. Walker the responsibility of carrying all our tickets and necessary cash, in gold dollars, upon her person. I had quite enough to do keeping the children in order, and exhausted myself walking them around and around the ship, and playing every sort of deck game there ever was in an effort to keep them out of mischief. If one of them should be missing for more than five minutes I almost had heart failure with fright, my mind's eye seeing him overboard and already a mere speck in the ocean. My frantic roundups greatly entertained the remaining two scamps. Fortunately this did not happen more than twice a day so my nerves, though stretched, were still in fair condition when we arrived in Vancouver. Here Mrs. Walker found a cable waiting for her from her father Colonel Goodman, advising us to delay the journey to New York as infantile paralysis had reached epidemic proportions in that city.[16]

Duly grateful for this warning she arranged that we stay a few days in Vancouver, where we did nothing much except to recuperate from the voyage and plan what to do next. It was decided to carry on to Seattle and spend some weeks there, so a suite was booked on the St. Paul and Milwaulkee line and even though I was getting used to travelling first class with the Walkers, never have I travelled in such comfort. In Seattle we made the New Washington Hotel our home from home,[17] but we were barely settled in before Mrs. Walker retired to bed as a result of eating too much crab, to which she was devoted. Well meaning as usual I put a notice on her door "DO NOT ENTER." "What's she got—smallpox?" enquired the chambermaid nervously, so I thought I had better change the notice to "DO NOT DISTURB." It was a few days before I was able to leave her and take the boys out for an airing as the poor kids were very bored with their enforced inactivity. While we were in the Bon Marché stores[18] an assistant noticed that young Donald was sporting his Boy Scout hat.

"Are you going to the big meeting?" she smiled at him.

"What meeting?" asks Donald, full of interest, as were Dick and Jack.

I explained that we had just come from China and did not know anything about anything. The girl then told us the Seattle Boy Scouts were being presented with the Colours, and it promised to be quite an occasion. "Why don't you take your boys along?" she suggested, and gave us details of where to go and how to get there. That sounded like a good idea to us so, after excavating their complete Scout uniforms from our trunks, we went to the meeting at the Bon Marché park the same afternoon. We, or should I say, *they*, created a real sensation amongst their fellow Scouts and, if the Seattle newspaper concerned does not object to me quoting from their report, here it is.

BOY SCOUTS FROM HONGKONG HERE

Yesterday the Seattle Boy Scouts, for the first time, saw the regalia of a British Boy Scout. Likewise three little fellows a long way from home and their patrol saw also for the first time the military costume of the American scout. Richard G. Walker, 13,

John G. Walker, 11, and Donald G. Walker, 7, sons of William Bradley Walker, manager of the Standard Oil Company at Hongkong, came out to join their brother scouts at the flag ceremony yesterday. They cheered and saluted with the rest, for they are Americans, although they belong to a British scout patrol called the Peak, after a section of the city in China. The little fellows are on their way to live with their grandfather, Col. T.C. Goodman, paymaster of the United States Army stationed at New York. [They] were accompanied by their mother and Mrs. J.G. Lyth, of Hongkong.

They are staying in Seattle for a while because of the infantile epidemic in New York. Richard is leader of his patrol. John is a second-class scout and little Donald is only a tenderfoot. Yesterday they were dressed in the English regalia—a blouse instead of the tight fitting coats of the American scout, and short knee breeches, full at the bottom.

"They seem to think our stockings very odd," said the oldest boy, "but it is impossible to wear them above the knee on account of the heat." Each boy had a kerchief in the colors of his patrol around his neck and each hat had a chin strap, neither of which are worn in this country. They wear their troop colors on the shoulders and carry a whistle on a lanyard with the troop colours.

They were invited to lead the scouts' march through the streets to the Orpheum Theatre, where they were the guests of the Wilkes Stock Company at the matinée,[19] which left me tagging along with the rabble in the rear but, on arrival, I was included in and sat with them surrounded by scouts on all sides.

VISITORS INTERVIEW ACTRESS

Between acts at the Orpheum the youngsters from Hongkong having expressed a keen desire to go backstage and meet the leading woman, Miss Phoebe Hunt, their request was granted. Miss Hunt became so interested in the chat with the scouts from faraway China that there was a curtain call wait for her.

The theatre manager took the boys on stage to show their uniforms to the audience, and to tell their story. They got a great reception, so much so that the manager asked me if they could give a repeat performance for the evening show. Mrs. Walker was delighted when we got back to the hotel and told her how famous we were becoming in Seattle, and not only gave her consent to the manager's request but came along with us. She was so proud to see her sons applauded on the stage and, truth to tell, so was I. Although the boys were pretty thrilled with themselves I must hand it to them that it did not give them swelled heads.

But my other most prominent memory of Seattle is not so pleasant, and that was to quote again, "one of the most severe electrical storms the city has ever experienced," and believe me it was one of the worst in my experience too. We were all scared out of our wits but I had to act brave in front of the children but what an effort it cost me, who was always petrified of the smallest rumble of thunder, and I still am.

It started about five-thirty one afternoon, becoming very dark suddenly and then, with a crash that shook the hotel, it got cracking. Wow! The ripping zig-zag lightning and the incessant violent thunder claps subdued even the young daredevil Jack. We saw the lightning run along the telephone wires until it hit the hotel dynamo, plunging us into even greater gloom, although I was rather pleased in one way as the boys could not see my frightened face. When at last it was all over we discovered we were not the only ones to suffer. A thunderbolt had stripped bare the steeple of the German Evangelical Lutheran Church, Terry Avenue and Stewart Street,[20] but in some miraculous way the cross atop the steeple remained untouched. We went to see it and were suitably awed by the bizarre sight. There was a lot of damage in the city caused by the torrential rains flooding the sewers, and we heard that a street had caved in, though whether this was true or false I never knew. I do know that the whole episode put me more off storms than ever.

After some weeks we moved on to Chicago intending to stay there with some friends of the Walker family, but a letter was awaiting us there from New York to say that the worst of the polio epidemic had passed over so we continued on to New York, where we settled thankfully into the Iroquois Hotel, 49 West 44th Street,[21] until a suitable apartment could be found. It seemed an awfully long time since we had left Hong Kong. Every morning, while at this hotel, Donald and I went to the Automat for breakfast. I don't know who got more fun out of putting in the dimes and watching the doors fly open, him or me. About evens I would say.

Mrs. Walker soon found an apartment in The Chautauqua, West End Avenue, a handsome twelve-storey building which had every conceivable luxury; from our windows we could see the Hudson and, as it was situated between Riverside Drive and Central Park, entertaining my charges simplified, especially when the snow came to stay. None of the children had ever seen snow before, and young Donald would eat it off the window sills like ice cream, but as our apartment was on the top floor I soon put a stop to this. What a time we had sleighing on Riverside Drive and, greatly daring, I actually learned to skate in Central Park. And how we all loved the little squirrels, so tame that they helped themselves to nuts from our pockets. Oh, there was such a lot to see and do in New York, the milling throngs in the subways and the buildings that reached up to the sky, the hustle and bustle of the city crept into my blood insidiously.

Before the two eldest boys went off to school it was my job to see that they enjoyed themselves. In doing this I was having a whale of a time myself. We went to hear Caruso sing at the Opera House, *and* Madame Tetrazzini.[22] Who ever heard more divine voices? Certainly not I. Madame Tetrazzini interrupted her own performance to put on a record of Caruso, and this struck me as a rather wonderful thing to do for I had always understood great names did not like to share the limelight. I must have been very fortunate for Pavlova, too, was in New York at that time and I saw her dance at the Hippodrome.[23] Dance is too poor a word, rather did she float like thistledown across the stage in a moonlit dream. I knew then I should never see such beauty again, nor have I.

Then there was Annette Kellermann, the Physical Culture teacher, playing at the Lyceum Theatre, in *The Daughter of the Gods*.[24] Her measurements were given out to the audience as that of the perfect woman, not merely the three vital statistics of today but those of her whole anatomy, neck, arms, wrists, ankles, et cetera. The foyer was crowded with artists all longing to be given a chance to add to the already many very wonderful portraits of her. The boys were movie mad and so we saw innumerable films on Broadway. Mary Pickford and Douglas Fairbanks were our heroine and hero, and *20,000 Leagues Under the Sea* had us in a whirl of fantasy for weeks afterwards.[25]

When, finally, Jack and Dick departed to Kingsley School in Essex Fells,[26] I missed them sadly and poor little Donald and his mother were completely lost. The picture postcards I got from them showed no such loss on their part, they were far too absorbed in marking pleasures of the school with various "X's" to demonstrate where they slept, studied, had meals, and so on.

America had by this time entered the War[27] but everything seemed to carry on quite normally nonetheless, but every letter I wrote to Am I felt would be my last as New York was so full of Germans; I thought they would blow us up, particularly as one rumour led us to believe that some had been caught, just in time, in an attempt to cut off New York's water supply. I was also resigned to the fact that my proposed trip home to England was off as no more bookings were being taken across the Atlantic. If only I had crossed this pond I should have done the round trip. A Captain Rice, who was a friend of the Walkers, was the first American to sink a German U-boat and, on his return to New York, he was given a tremendous reception.[28] I can see Mrs. Walker now, dressed in a beautiful yellow taffeta frock, as she set out to join in the festivities.

But from there onwards everything went very much wrong for me. It started with Mrs. Walker falling ill with Vincent Angina,[29] so little Donald was sent to his grandmother's while I devoted my full attention to nursing her through this. She got better pretty soon and Donald came back but as he did not seem too well I took him to sleep in my room so that he would not disturb his mother. A morning or two later I woke up with a shockingly bad throat and, on looking at it in the mirror, was horrified to find it covered in repulsive spots. Donald ran in to tell his Mummy who took one look and summoned a doctor. He took a swab from my throat for examination, telling me to remain in bed; the same evening I developed stomach pains so acute that the doctor, back again, suspected appendicitis and my throat as diphtheria. Straightaway I was bustled off in an ambulance to the Willard Parker Hospital[30] as a precautionary measure. He was right. I had diphtheria, and thirty-five thousand units of anti-toxin were pushed into me. I felt dreadful, and afraid and alone. The appendix was also confirmed but nothing could be done about that until I recovered from the diphtheria, and then just to complicate matters further I got jaundice as well. It was a long time later that I learned they did not expect me to last out the night, and had sent a message to that effect to Mrs. Walker's mother, who had then phoned her daughter.

"Are you feeling very strong?" she asked.

"Why?" replied Mrs. Walker, not feeling strong at all.

"Mrs. Lyth is not expected to live until the morning," warned Mrs. Goodman.

Poor Mrs. Walker. There she was only getting over her own illness, and as Donald was not well either she could not leave him to get down to the hospital. After contacting her sister, who sent her fiancé along to the hospital, she could only phone for news of me every hour or so. In order for the unfortunate young man to be admitted, they told me to say he was my brother. He arrived at midnight only to be informed I was in a coma so he was sent home again, which was just as well as I don't suppose we would have had a very satisfactory deathbed scene, being total strangers! In spite of all this I made a good recovery, and was getting ready to leave the hospital when measles broke out in the ward. None of the children were allowed home but some of the adults, including me, they released; I cheated a little by saying I thought I'd had measles anyway.

A Mrs. Brown with whom I had become friendly while in New York (we had met through a letter of introduction I had brought with me from Hong Kong), invited me to convalesce at her home and that was where I went.

Although she had lived in New York for twenty-five years, Mrs. Brown was still as English as the day she was born, and proudly flew a Union Jack over her front door, a sight for sore eyes I thought as I stepped out of the taxi. She could not have been kinder to me but after eleven days I became ill again. Temperature 103. The doctor was called and back I went to hospital, the Roosevelt this time,[31] for an appendix operation. I spent that night in a surgical ward of twenty-eight patients only to wake up in the morning covered in spots. I had measles! Panic ensued. I was out of that ward back in the Willard Parker Hospital quicker than a shot from a gun and there I remained until I was no longer infectious. Once more Mrs. Brown, brave woman, took me into her home to gather strength for the appendix operation which had still to come and, this time, all went according to plan except that they also operated for adhesions on my gall bladder which I had not expected at all.

All this took up quite a lot of my time and I often wondered if I should ever get back to Hong Kong alive; as for Am, he was going quickly crazy as he heard of each new development and tried to keep up with my rapid changes of address. The Walkers kept him informed and, indeed, on several occasions when he was about to apply for compassionate leave to America it was only to hear that I was out of danger by the next post. The mail, of course, took so long that each crisis was over by the time he got to hear of it. He got confused and, in the end, incredulous. No woman, he thought, could have so many different things wrong with her.

By the time I was ready to stagger to a convalescent home in White Plains, Mrs. Walker was in the process of moving out to a pretty little house in Pelham,[32] for her husband was on his way to join her on a vacation stipulating, however, that he would not spend it in New York City. Before leaving he promised Am he would send me back to Hong Kong just as soon as I was fit to travel. After two weeks in White Plains I felt pretty good. Mrs. Brown insisted that I remain with her until my arrangements were made to go home, and as Donald was due to start school I felt Mrs. Walker would no longer need me, and she agreed to release me. After three months in and out of hospitals I was feeling depressed but I bucked up a lot after booking my passage. I guess I must have had a bit of an aesthetic look about me for when I called on the British Consul he asked me if I was a missionary going to China! He should have seen me enjoying myself on Coney Island[33] with the Browns. Boy, what a place. Then I had a wonderful trip up the Hudson River with an English lady who had been my neighbour in the Roosevelt Hospital; she was a secretary to a cotton firm in Georgia, and did she appreciate having another Englishwoman to talk to. I was so thrilled to see West Point and the home of George Washington.[34]

I bade a sad farewell to little Donald, Mr. and Mrs. Walker, the Browns, and other friends I had made before leaving New York Central for Montreal on the first leg of my journey. I had a twenty-four hour wait in Montreal, most of which I spent with a lady whom I met in a park; as soon as we discovered we were both wasting time between trains we joined forces and had a darned good time doing the town, ending up by going to St. George's Church where the bells were ringing "Abide with Me"[35] and then, to my joy, "God Save the King." It seemed a near miracle to hear my national anthem again.

The Canadian Pacific train left Montreal en route for Vancouver late that night and, knowing it to be a five-day journey, I had the forethought to take a skipping rope with me; at the various stops I jumped out and skipped madly to relieve my stiff limbs. A lot of my fellow passengers thought it a wonderful idea and begged a loan of my skipping rope. I soon discovered that travelling second class was not *quite* the same luxury as when one had a suite and the service that went with it. On the other hand, although it was nice to have known how the other half lived, I found advantage in the friendliness all around me. There was a Mr. Wagg and his daughter, for instance, who joined the train at Moose Jaw.[36] They were going on a fishing holiday, and he teased his daughter by telling everyone that he was taking her along so that she could see some trees, for she was born and bred in prairie land. No doubt he was pulling my leg a little for it seemed strange to me that anyone could not have seen a *tree*. They would have me share their picnic basket and would not let me miss any of the glories of the Canadian Rockies and, indeed, the constant grandeur of these magnificent mountains held me spellbound. At one point the train stopped so that the passengers could get out to watch the wondrous spectacle of a great rush of waters into a huge canyon (darned if I can think of the name[37]), at such force that it looked as if it was boiling in the depths below.

When at long last we arrived in Vancouver I booked in grandly at the Vancouver Hotel only to find, next day, that the longshoremen were on strike, and my ship could not sail. Oh well, I thought philosophically, this gives me time to look up Mrs. Milne (another lady to whom I had a letter of introduction), and a charming person she proved to be with an equally charming family; they entertained me royally, taking me swimming, surf riding, and playing tennis, the latter giving me the first opportunity of using my tennis racket since I got to the American continent. They also took me to the Vancouver Club,[38] and this I enjoyed tremendously as I gathered it was an exclusive spot. This sort of thing went on for a week each day of which I called at the Canadian Pacific Office for news of the strike, but the strike went on and on and my funds went down and down! I was getting worried. Should I cable Am for more money, or dare I waste the money I had in sending a cable? I moved from the hotel to the Y.W.C.A. Hostel (from the sublime to the ridiculous), to conserve my cash without mentioning the fact to my friends. I knew they would have had me move in with them, but I also knew their house was pretty full already and, in any case, I felt I must be outwearing my welcome. Then, one morning, as I left the C.P.O. a clerk came running after me.

"Are you Mrs. Lyth from New York?" he shouted.

"Yes," I replied, puzzled.

"We've had a cable from Mr. W.B. Walker asking us to pay your hotel until your ship sails!"

Those few words were worth all the tea in China to me, to use a fairly apt phrase. I was sorely tempted to return to the hotel but pride prevailed, and I was glad I did not have to take up Mr. Walker's kind offer but managed to eke out on my own few dollars, but, oh my, it was good to have that promise behind me. How grateful I was to them for following my journey in their thoughts. It was three weeks in all before the strike was over.

When the *Monteagle*[39] did sail there were a hundred and fifty missionaries on board her. On the trip we lost a day due to our crossing the 180th (I don't know how this works out but it does),[40] and the day happened to be a Sunday. This the missionaries would not have at all so they used the Saturday for a Sunday, and picked on me to choose the hymn for their service. I thought myself slyly clever in choosing "Jesus Shall Reign *Where'er* the Sun"![41]

The Pacific was kind to me again and I enjoyed the voyage, and became very friendly with one of the stewardesses. When we docked in Yokohama she asked me if I would like to visit No. 9, a noted Geisha house.[42]

"Yes," I said cautiously, "if I don't have to do anything!"

She laughed and told me I would be quite safe so we went, and I gazed enraptured at the pretty Japanese girls and the charming way in which they served the men with refreshments. I was impressed and almost wished I was a man myself. The only faux pas I made was to go into the gentlemen's toilet in mistake for the females. The coolie ran towards me and wrung his hands in dismay.

"No, no," he cried in horror, "Missee no belong here proper!"

Missee got out again very quickly. Once more I tried to imprint forever in my memory the charms of the Inland Sea for, somehow, I could not see myself travelling this way again. Then at long last there was Hong Kong's beautiful harbour opening wide its arms in welcome, and there was my beloved Am with his arms, too, waiting to embrace me. All we wanted after that was to be left very much alone, but our friends insisted on making a welcome home party for me, and this lasted the larger part of the night!

Chapter 4

Am's coming-home present to me was a neat little house inside the Military Hospital compound which, somehow or other, he had managed to get allocated to us; he was making quite sure that I would not have far to go should I develop any more diseases. Seriously, he was surprised to find me looking so well having expected something more on the lines of a death's head. My, but it was good to be back again with him. All I wanted to do was take life easy and devote all my time to my husband for a change. But this, needless to say, did not last long. I soon got the urge to be up and doing, so on the strength of my experiences with the Walker boys, I applied to the Diocesan Boys' School[43] for an Assistant Mistress's post, *and* I got it. I was delighted to be surrounded by children again, and the comforting feel of a wage packet of my own was another pleasing factor.

The boys were European, Chinese, and Eurasian. I liked getting them when they just started school so that I could see the results of my own teaching. Neither pupils nor teachers were allowed to use Pidgin English in school and we were periodically switched around so that the children would not speak English with any particular accent. Often when there was such a move and I lost touch with my little new boys I got so livid I could have spat. It took me a little while getting used to adding a year to the ages of the Chinese children who are reckoned a year old when born.

The headmistress remarked casually one day that she thought it strange that I should work in a Diocesan School.

"Why?" I asked, a bit taken aback.

"Well," she said, "you go to St. Joseph's Roman Catholic Church every Sunday, don't you?" (Naturally everyone knew everything about everyone in the Colony.)

I replied with great dignity, "I go to hear my husband sing in the choir but," I added warmly, "if you are born in a stable it doesn't mean you are a horse!"

There were no more references to my churchgoings, and indeed I still had no thoughts of becoming a Roman Catholic and Am never urged it upon me, and I soon became a familiar face about the school. The boys were pretty easy to handle on the whole although I had my difficult moments. There was the morning a hand went up requesting permission to speak.

"Please, Mum, there is ink on your dress!"

That was putting it mildly. The back of my dress was ink from top to bottom. I ordered them to down tools and then counted ten very slowly to myself before uttering a word.

"Some very naughty little boy has inked my dress," I announced, and drew a deep breath. "If he will confess I will forgive him. I give you five minutes."

I felt pretty magnanimous at this offer but as no one took advantage of it I told them I must send for the Headmaster. He tried to find the culprit with a similar lack of result. The punishment he decided upon was that my class would be held in his room for the next week. I was flabbergasted. Just who he thought he was punishing I don't know but I do know I suffered more than my pupils over it, stammering and stuttering my way through the lessons under the head's eagle eye was sheer agony. I was considerably mollified however to find this little farewell note to his desk in one of the children's exercise books; indeed so much did I like it that I sank so low as to steal it from his book.

To My Dear Desk

I am very sorry to say that I cannot stay with you little longer, because some boys who in this class were naughty make Mrs. Lyth's dress dirty with ink and she reported to our headmaster. On Saturday morning Mrs. Lyth was absent with angry for those boys make her dress dirty so our headmaster come and give us punishment to stay in school-room on Monday, and I must leave you. I can't any excuse to headmaster, so I must close my letter and leave. Goodbye, see you again when some body take you to six or five classroom.

From your Owner.

But I had not learned my lesson yet. I had one class of thirty-five boys for reading and dictation; they were twelve and thirteen year olds, and were always given time to study the harder words before dictation but, when checking the exercise books, I found that the boy whose average score was ten out of fifty had suddenly merited one hundred per cent, which was clearly impossible. I called him to my desk.

"How did you come to do so well?" I asked curiously.

"Don't know, Mum," he replied.

Whereupon his next door neighbour sprang up, "Please, Mum, he wrote it down when we were learning the hard words."

I felt something had to be done and, as we were not allowed to punish the children ourselves, I gave the child a note to take to the Headmaster. I really felt like giving a thick ear to the one who had sneaked on him but restrained myself. After a while the Head came in followed by the culprit.

"I found this boy standing in my room, Mrs. Lyth. What does he want?"

"Why, he has a note for you," I replied in surprise, so I was forced to explain what it was all about, and asked the boy what he had done with it.

"I've torn it up," he muttered pathetically.

The Headmaster became very stern. "Boys, listen to me. I hate cheats. I'm going to send this boy home now and he is not coming back to this school any more."

I did not think he meant it but, next day, when the boy's guardians brought him back the Headmaster was obdurate about the whole episode. There and then I resolved never again to have a boy expelled from my class but to deal, somehow, with any future problems by myself.

It was during a school holiday that a most appalling tragedy shook Hong Kong to its foundations.[44] It was Race Week, a very festive occasion in the Colony, when the racecourse at Wong Nai Chung Valley, also called Happy Valley, was packed to overflowing day after day. The bell had rung for the first race after tiffin[45] on the Wednesday when, with no preliminary warning, the whole row of Chinese betting booths and matsheds suddenly collapsed, folding together like the bellows of a concertina, and trapping a seething mass of punters. Everyone rushed to the rescue although many of the victims were already pushing their way through the broken bamboo walls and roofs of leaves; there was confusion and cries of fright from the men, women, and children, but no panic... until the first flames flashed out from one of the matsheds. The fire spread with lightening speed and screams of terror came bursting from all throats—a mad spasm shook through the devastated area and all those who could, ran, and those who could not were flung to the ground and trampled to death, mostly small children and women; the police, soldiers, and civilians fought to rescue any who could be reached before the blaze threw them back to watch, sickened, pinned, and trapped fellow beings burn to death in front of their eyes. (Am saw a little Japanese girl praying as she waited for the flames to reach her.)

The Fire Brigade came in to stop the fire from spreading after the Golf Club had been gutted, but the recovery of the bodies went on until the late hours of the night. Over 675 bodies were laid out on the Race Course.

Thank God, I had not gone to the races that day but, in the early afternoon, the first rumours that all was not well reached me so I checked at the hospital for confirmation, knowing Am was acting as a steward at the races. They told me he was helping in the rescue work but that I must not worry. They did not say just how bad it was.

When there was still no sign of Am at midnight I ran down to the Police Station. They told me there was nothing I could do but go home and wait and, on no account, was I to go to Happy Valley. I spent the rest of the night walking the floor and worrying myself sick. Am came back at five in the morning, exhausted, speechless, and at least ten years older.

Nearly all the dead were Chinese though this would not have been so but for the fact that Spotted Fever[46] was raging in Hong Kong, and all Europeans had been advised not to enter the Chinese matsheds. Our soldiers normally used them as the Tote, as five dollars minimum stake was beyond their pockets. This time they evaded the issue by using Chinese coolies as go-betweens. It was a long time before we could dismiss the horrifying death roll from our minds; the only explanation ever offered was that it must have been the work of thieves who had partly sawn through the bamboo pole supports, but that they had not reckoned on fire breaking out.

When Swatow, about three hundred miles from Hong Kong, was reduced to ruins by an earthquake we felt the tremors,[47] although as I set the table for tea I did not know what it was when the cups and saucers started dancing, and the pictures falling from the walls. I just goggled. My neighbours shouted to me "Come out!" which I did only to be told it was an earthquake. I charged back to fetch Am out of the bath, dragging him outside clad only in a towel. However, we need not have worried for ourselves, there was no damage to speak of on the Peak[48] although there were a few minor displacements lower down.

When news came that the war was over the Headmaster closed the school, and Am phoned through to know what was going on as his office, like the rest, had shut down so we met at the Astor Hotel[49] and proceeded to celebrate. Our teetotal ways went by the board. We went from one hotel to another and Club after Club; we were invited to dinner in the Hong Kong Hotel so went off home to change but, on the way, I had to ask the chair coolie to put me down I felt so ill, and so ashamed. After a rest Am said "Come, get up. It's time we dressed."

"Carry on," I groaned miserably, "leave me here to die!"

He did, and came home at five a.m. next morning none the worse for wear.

Am, now a Sergeant, was a little surprised to find he had been awarded the Meritorious Medal for "valuable services connected with the War." However, with the war over it did mean that it would be easier to get to England, and Am urged me to take the first opportunity that arose to go home and build up my strength before returning. He was not convinced that I was fully recovered from all my illnesses and, as he had hope of obtaining a civilian job in Hong Kong, if the Army would release him, he hoped to settle there. A chance did come. I signed on as Nanny to the children of a Major's family, who were returning to England. But, before I left, I managed a visit to Macau Island in South China, a real gambling spot where Fan-Tan was the game on which to lose your money.[50] I did not win a fortune but I did not do too badly either much to Am's annoyance who could not win a cent. I enjoyed the two hour boat journey and, coming back, we all got very jolly on Samshu, a Chinese rice spirit which we thought disgusting stuff but it certainly caused us to be merrier than ever before in our lives.

For the third time I waved farewell to Am from a ship's deck as I sailed for the United Kingdom on the *Sphinx*[51] with the Major and his family. Travelling with us was a rather unusual passenger in the person of a Chilean lady; she was being deported from America for shooting her husband! She was accompanied by her sister who was minding her little boy and I, ever curious, had many talks with the sister, and got the whole story after a while.

The girl's husband was a pretty nasty specimen and, at seven o'clock one morning, he returned home from some debauch to find his wife waiting for him with a revolver instead of a kiss, and that was that. The American courts had, apparently, decided she had suffered provocation and deportation was their sentence. The girl, for she was not much more, dressed very quietly, always wore dark glasses, and was rarely to be seen without gloves. She aroused much controversy. So pale was her complexion that many of the passengers swore she bathed in milk, but I'm darned sure she could not have done it while on board at least. She was a beautiful woman, so pale, with enormous dark eyes and the serene expression of a Madonna despite all she had gone through. She rested each afternoon and at night, dressed in her favourite black, she was the envy of every woman, and not a man could take his eyes from her. I have never seen a woman so petite and lovely.

After calling at Haiphong, Saigon, and Colombo, we passed through Suez in the night. Our soldiers were on the banks.

"What's the name of your ship?" they shouted.

"The *Sphinx*," we yelled back.

"Where are you going?" came the next question.

"Home!" we told them.

"Throw us a rope then," they cried wistfully, and we felt a little bit mean that it was us and not them who were on our way home.

The next night my mistress came to my cabin. "Have you got your money and a big coat handy?" she asked me.

"Whatever for?" I was amazed.

"Because we're going through the Straits of Messina where all those mines were laid!"

This information did not rattle me much. What will be will be was always my motto. Still is for that matter. I saw Mount Etna and was a bit disappointed not to see it pouring out lava as I had pictured it. Then, a few days from Marseilles, a French soldier on our boat died of war wounds and was buried at sea. The Captain stopped the ship and most of the passengers attended the service but, somehow, I could not bring myself to do this. It seemed far too sad to think the boy was only such a little way from home when he died.

We disembarked at Marseilles, the Major's family being of the same mind as myself about the Bay of Biscay, and the idea was to travel to Paris and continue on to London from there. Next day, however, while visiting his bank the Major met his family doctor who persuaded him to let us all travel on his ambulance train to England via Le Havre. And so we did but I felt cheated at not seeing Paris after all. We had a filthy crossing to Southampton and I was sick as a dog,[52] but the children did not mind a bit which was just as well I suppose. We went on to Bournemouth where I agreed to stay on with them awhile until I knew more about what Am was doing.

My sisters were delighted to see me looking so well and we had a joyous reunion, but they cooled off considerably when they discovered a very changed Jiz from the quiet little thing they remembered. I liked life now, swam, played tennis, whist and bridge, and I *danced*!

Unfortunately Am was not able to fix anything although he was offered a good job with a good salary; but the Army insisted that he complete his twenty-one years service to the day, which was another year and eleven months. How disappointed we were but there was not a thing we could do about it. I was getting ready to re-join him when he cabled me that he was being posted back to England within a few months. I left the Major's family and went to stay with Snow who, now married, was living in Wheathampstead, a Hertfordshire village.[53] It was a pleasant interlude for me and did much to settle me down to English life again. Looking through her window one morning she called my attention to a car going by, driven by a white-bearded man.

"There goes that old man[54] from Ayot St. Lawrence. He writes books."

"Oh yes," I murmured vaguely, giving a perfunctory glance and immediately forgot him. I had not the remotest idea of where Ayot St. Lawrence was, nor who the man might be. Even if I did not know it then this was the very first time I set eyes on George Bernard Shaw. Another few years were to pass before I saw him again.

When I finally knew the date of Am's return to England, and to Brighton[55] in particular, I set about getting our bits and pieces out of store and installed in a flat which I had managed to get, but the firm would not part with the goods without Am's signature; mine was no good at all. Nor was that of the Major with whom I had come to England. Tired of waiting for Am's reply to my letter I went to a solicitor and swore on affidavit to the effect that I was Mrs. Lyth, and had my husband's authority to remove the goods. Eventually they agreed to let me have them but, on hearing the charges that had accrued, I thought I had better leave them after all. When he did [reply] we both decided the stuff could stay there for good rather than pay the frightful bill, and there they remained and probably still do.

He arrived in August, a hot one it was that year, and what did he do but collapse with the heat. He was terribly ill but all I could do was laugh my head off unsympathetically. All those years in Hong Kong but he had to wait until he got to Brighton to get sunstroke! Poor old Am. He never lived that down.

He still had the wanderlust, and I was aiding and abetting him this time when he volunteered to wind up his service in Africa. He went for his medical examination but was amazed when the doctor would not pass him fit. He then gave Am a letter for his Commanding Officer asking that "this N.C.O. should be admitted to hospital as soon as possible." Am's heart was not up to standard. It came as a profound shock to us both that there should be anything wrong with him.

"I feel perfectly well," Am comforted me. "There's nothing wrong with me and I'm not going to hospital."

Nor would he. Not even his C.O. could coerce him into it, and they were good friends of long standing.

"Just pretend you haven't seen the letter," suggested Am to him.

"I can't do that," replied the C.O. but he promised to sleep on it. Next morning he still insisted that the doctor's orders should be obeyed.

"No!" Am was adamant. "Can't you post me then?" asked my husband, suggesting an alternative, and that was how he got away with it.

We were posted to Maresfield, eighteen miles from Brighton, a lovely country spot and there we finished out his last eleven months in the Army. Here we enjoyed life to the full, playing tennis violently and leading a hectic social life; gradually we forgot all about the insinuation that all was not well with Am.

At last, after twenty-one years as a soldier, the day came for his release. We were civilians. We were on our own. What to do next? Not to worry, let's take a holiday first to get acclimatised we thought. How were we to know that life was not quite so easy, nor jobs to be found like ripe plums just waiting to be plucked. We didn't.

Chapter 5

Free from his uniform Am, now forty-four, was full of the joys of spring, and insisted upon us holidaying with his sister in Yorkshire[56] for a while before picking up a job. This innocent outlook on life soon got shattered. It was 1922, and a worse time we could not have picked to take up the threads of civilian life for it was a time of national depression, and mass unemployment was spreading rapidly. Seven weary and very frightening months went by before he succeeded in finding work of any kind. Every day of that time was spent in searching for a clerical post, the only work he knew, but office jobs were unobtainable. To eke out our finances I went to nurse an aunt of his who was ill whilst Am remained in Whitby desperately seeking work of any kind, his small pension just permitting him to exist. At length we landed a joint job in a small preparatory school in Harrogate,[57] he as the odd job man and I the cook. We were chosen from 107 applicants which tells its own story. As we lived in the school we had no rent to pay but Am did not like to see me working so hard, and it was hard work cooking for all those boys. Eventually he found another job, this time as a gardener, to a convalescent home in Leeds.[58] There were 110 others who wanted the job too. A cottage went with this job as well as coal and wood and, of course, we grew our own vegetables so we began to feel positively rich, and began collecting some furniture on the never never.[59]

But there was one big snag. Am was not used to such heavy manual work and his exhaustion each night was terrible to see as he staggered home, barely able to raise one foot after the other. My heart sank at the sight of his poor white face. He never complained but neither did he protest when I went with him to the gardens to do what I could to help. For two years he laboured on, not hardening to it as he had hoped but growing steadily thinner and weaker, and all the time he looked anxiously for a sitting down job hoping one day to strike lucky. He never did. This was rock bottom in our married life, and, maybe for that reason, I began to feel drawn towards Am's religion although he himself continued to take it lightly, only going to Mass to sing in the choir, and he did nothing to encourage me. However, my feelings were strong and I took instructions from the Parish priest, persevering until I was finally accepted and baptised a Roman Catholic. It was only then that I finally accepted the fact that, in the eyes of Rome, we were not married at all but living in sin! The only remedy was for us to be married again, at this late date, by a Roman Catholic priest and this we did but, after the solemnity of the wedding ceremony, we felt more than a little foolish when we had to undergo the leg pulling and meaning jokes familiar to newly weds for the second time in our joint lives. However, my enthusiasm for my adopted religion weaned Am back to the fold more successfully than any priest had been able to do. We found a lot of comfort in this and in each other at this time.

No longer did we play our well-loved tennis for Am had no spare energy, only wanting to spend the evenings gathering together enough strength for the following day. Our only relaxation was an occasional game of bridge. In time we managed to save enough money to pay our fares to Hartlepool[60] for a holiday with my brother-in-law but when it was time to return I fell ill with food poisoning, so Am went home alone. On reaching the cottage he found a newspaper tucked under the door knocker with a note attached from the editor, who was a friend of his, telling him to answer the advertisement he had marked. It was for a steward and stewardess to a Conservative Club in Bradford.[61] Am grabbed pen and paper and wrote at once, and when I got home a few days later I was met by the wonderful news that we had been called for an interview. Not daring to hope, and trying to look as much like a steward and stewardess as possible though we were none too sure what this should be, we went.

There were half a dozen other couples there, all looking a darn sight more confident of themselves than we felt; the women were flashily made up whereas I was as natural as God had made me. The interview itself appeared to go well and the Secretary followed us out saying, "Cheer up, Mr. Lyth, I think you'll be hearing from us," and within a few days we did. The letter said the job was ours and could we let them have a Fidelity Bond of £50. That soon brought us down to earth again. We had not got £50 or £5 either. Am's brother came to the rescue with a loan of £35 and this the Club accepted, the rest to be deducted from our joint salary of £3 10s. a week. This does not sound like a lot but it was riches to us when we realised that accommodation, light, and coal were all free. And, when we settled in, my grocery bills were practically non-existent more often than not as we were invited to join in at most of the lunch and dinner functions held at the Club.

Stewardship was child's play to Am after the heartbreaking labour of gardening, although he still tired quickly despite giving the appearance of a hale and hearty man. As for me, I revelled in the social life, having a maid to keep our flat clean and tidy whilst I devoted my time to the Club, as well as helping Am to run the bar. For a long time we could hardly believe this was really us, and put all we knew into the job for fear we might lose it. We were given a little dog by one of the members; so well mannered was she that I called her Lady and she became part of the establishment.

Everything went swimmingly for about fourteen months when, suddenly, Am fell ill. The doctor diagnosed it as congestion of the lungs and had him removed to hospital on a stretcher. It was then I remembered Am telling me that his father and mother, uncles and aunts, had all died of cancer. Terrified that he, too, might be heading that way I begged the doctor to look for a growth, thinking that if it was found in time his life could be saved. There was no growth, for which I thanked God, but I was warned that it would be a long time before he would be well again. He was in the hospital a month and then went down to my sister in Wheathamstead to convalesce. I carried on as well as I could, getting in someone to run the bar for me, and I was so happy when Am came back looking rested and well. It did not last. Within three months he was ill again. His heart was now pinpointed as the cause of the trouble, a Tropical Heart they called it.

"How stupid we've been," I sobbed to him. "Why didn't we listen when they told you to go to the hospital in the Army?"

But he would not let me worry and swore that another month's rest would see him right. He went again to Wheathamstead but when he came back the Club Secretary came to see me.

"Am is no better," he whispered, and I knew him to be right.

We struggled along for a further three months but it was no good. I had to help him climb the stairs and, at night, to prop him upright so that he could get his breath. We had to send in our resignations.

Now it was up to me to earn our living for Am was told he must not exert himself in any way. I wrote to my sister Snow and, again, she came to our rescue by finding a cottage to rent in Wheathamstead. There we went and back I went to my sure fire money spinner, cooking. I took a job at a restaurant in Welwyn Garden City, about five miles away, where I was well paid and enjoyed the work but, after six months of it, I became afraid to leave Am alone all day and got a job locally so that I could be near him and yet still bring in some money. The days must have been long for him despite his pre-occupation as Secretary to the British Legion and Slate clubs,[62] and he was Cub Master to a pack of small boys who adored him. Granpa Cub they called him.

One day the lady for whom I was working remarked how hard my life must be running my own home, looking after Am, and working for her.

"Why don't you and your husband come to live here?" she asked me. "It would make things easier for you."

"But what am I to do with my home?" I said.

"Sell it," she replied.

"Never!" I gasped, thinking of the struggle we had to get our furniture together.

"Would you sub-let it then?" she suggested.

This sounded a good idea so we did, for twelve shillings a week, and moved into this kind lady's large house where I had more time to devote to Am. I had to dress and bath him by this time for he could not even bend to tie his own shoes. The astonishing part of his illness was that he looked so well but it was as much as he could do to take our little dog for a short walk. He gave up acting as secretary to his clubs, and spent most of his time doing various newspaper competitions in the hope he would win enough money for us to retire. Poor Am, what a miserable time it was for him. Then we saw an advertisement for a postmaster to a small sub-office in a Hertfordshire village and, thinking he could cope with this with me there to help him, he applied for it.

For some reason we felt in our bones that we would get this job and, therefore, felt no surprise when a letter came inviting him to attend an interview in Ayot St. Lawrence. Although we lived a mere two and a half miles from there we had never even seen this village and to get there it meant biking or walking, so I insisted that Am went by taxi. He thought the meeting went well but did not think I would like the cottage, saying I need not bother going to see it. But when we got on the short list of likely tenants and were called again for [an] interview, I made sure that I went along too.

So tiny a village was Ayot St. Lawrence that I did not realise we had passed through it until Am said, "That was it!" as we turned into the driveway to Ayot House, a big red brick house of fifty-odd rooms. There we met the Hon. Nall-Cain and his wife (who were later to become Lord and Lady Brocket),[63] and their agent. They took us to see the post office, an authentic Tudor, half-timbered cottage, with great oak beams in the ceilings and walls. It was small, only two bedrooms, the office, one living room and a kitchen, with a neat little garden running parallel to the village street. The small windows made it gloomy indoors, and the dull browns and greens of the interior decorations did nothing to lighten it.

"I think if I had this cottage I could make it pretty," Mrs. Nall-Cain remarked to me.

I looked upon it with new eyes after she had said this and I, too, suddenly saw its possibilities. The village itself looked utterly delightful in its early summer dress. The street, if you could call it such, was but a narrow road nestling beneath a tunnel of trees before ambling past the picturesque ruins of a church, a pretty cottage, the post office, and the old Inn beside it, before meandering through another archway of trees away down narrower and narrower lanes, not much wider than the taxi we rode in. Not a soul was to be seen. There was a hushed and peaceful air all about.

"We could be happy here, Am," I whispered to him, seeing ourselves growing old peacefully like the village itself.

"Yes, this is for us!" he smiled, but we had another week to wait until it was confirmed that it was indeed for us, as first the post office had to accept him for the job as postmaster, for that part was nothing to do with the Hon. Nall-Cain. Am's Army record quickly convinced the postal authorities of his capabilities and he was officially appointed. The cottage was redecorated for us in lighter colours, and the outside newly whitewashed before we moved in. With our furniture installed, and our pretty Japanese pictures reflecting light, it began to look attractive. My cherished Chinese silk square I had framed and hung over the big, recessed fireplace; strangely, the cockatoos in brilliant colours, the peacocks with their tails outstretched, the wild duck and heron flying over the delicate water lilies, all startlingly lovely against the pale blue background, blended well with the beams, and gave a light of its own to the room.

Shaw in Ayot St Lawrence (Chappelow 120)

Already Am seemed a new man with an aim in life and I loved to see him bubble over with plans for our future here. As soon as he realised that our stock was confined to £25 worth of stamps and postal orders he applied for a larger allocation and, realising that his salary of twelve shillings a week with five deducted for rent left us with only seven shillings for ourselves, he decided we could augment this by opening a grocery and sweet shop. The other goods for sale in the village were our stamps and beer from the Inn.

We started off by getting in £10 worth of stock on credit and awaited results with some trepidation. Slowly but surely the villagers began to buy from us, and the children were delighted to find sweets for sale in the post office. Am remembered his book-keeping and opened ledgers in his beautiful copperplate writing, teaching me how to keep the accounts straight.

He was quick, too, to cotton on to the fact that the charming old gentleman he had met in the village was none other than Mr. George Bernard Shaw who, he informed me, was a very famous man who wrote plays, and that the people we saw wandering about the village during weekends were all his followers. He liked Mr. Shaw's musical voice and his sparkling eyes, which looked full of mischief, and thought that he would like to try and read some of his works but we were busy getting our house in order and had little time to spare for reading. Both the post office and shop were so new to us that we were continually learning something fresh. Another idea Am had was to have the post office photographed for postcard reproduction with a view to selling it as a souvenir of Ayot and, if it was successful, to add other local points of interest.

Everything was beginning to sort itself out nicely and we dreamed away the lovely summer days in our happiness at being together in a home of our own, and at being self-supporting. In the golden evenings we strolled slowly through the natural parklands while our little dog, Lady, chased madly through a grass sea of waving buttercups, and the candles of the chestnut trees blew their blossoms away on the wind. The three lonely fir trees stood close together, swaying gently, bespattered with baby cones, and the green-roofed Grecian styled church across the meadow cuddled into the trees half circling it. This church was an unexpected sight in an English village. Hidden away it was, with its green copper roof and open pavilions on either side, it looked more like a Greek temple. We chuckled over the handed-down tale of how that church, known locally as the New Church although built in 1788, came to be there at all.

The Lord of the Manor, a Sir Lionel Lyde, did not like the view from his windows being obstructed by the original village church so he proceeded to pull it down, intending to build another at the other side of the park. Lords of the Manor could do pretty well what they liked in those olden days but, on this occasion, the Bishop got to hear of it and was livid with rage. He ordered Sir Lionel to stop his wanton destruction forthwith and to repair the damage already done. However, the church was already more than half down so Sir Lionel ignored the Bishop's request but sought to make amends by commissioning Nicholas Revett, the architect who designed London's St. Pancras Church, to produce one on similar lines for little Ayot St. Lawrence.

But this was not quite the end of the story for this same Lord's marriage was, apparently, a matter of constant regret to him and, as the church had joined them together in life, he thought the least it could do to make amends was to separate them in death. He, therefore, left explicit instructions that his tomb, and that of his wife, should be placed at opposite sides of the New Church and there they are to this day, a good thirty yards between their tombs![64]

The church he destroyed, known now as the Old Ruins, is but a shell although with its ivy covered walls it is a pretty sight. Americans in particular take a great fancy to it and aim cameras at it from all angles. Since the war ended they ask, "Was it bombed?" Of course I have to be truthful and say "No," which means an explanation so I tell them the story, and their incredulous faces are a joy to watch when I finish off by pointing out the New Church. "New Church? When did you say it was built?" I tell them again and they go away muttering "1788. That's new! *Seventeen eighty-eight!*"

Incidentally, one stained glass window was rescued from the Old Church and re-set in the Rectory where it is to this day and, although the house itself has been converted into flats, it is still known as the Old Rectory. However, as we assimilated local history, we gathered practically every other house in Ayot had been a rectory at one time or another. Following the Old Rectory a thatched cottage was used prior to the building of a proper rectory, to be known as the New Rectory and which in time came to be known as Shaw's Corner. (Indeed Mr. Shaw frequently received letters addressed to the Rev. B. Shaw!) When the New Rectory proved too large, a smaller house on the opposite corner was built for the purpose. That does not seem to have stayed a rectory for long either for, when the village school closed down for lack of pupils, the schoolhouse became the rectory which was the position when Am and I arrived. *Now* there is no rectory at all. It has moved to Ayot St. Peter[65] with which parish we are amalgamated. Having then neither school nor rectory the children go to Sunday school in the tap room[66] of the Inn.

Intriguing too was the story of the old manor house. Henry VIII was said to have used it as a hunting lodge, and had a nasty habit of shutting up Anne Boleyn, his current wife, in a windowless room whilst he was off enjoying himself. Whether this tale is true or false would be hard to tell, but that room is there and very dark it is too. I, for one, would not care to be imprisoned in it. Henry left his hat and Anne's shoes as a sort of royal seal when he bestowed the house, and these souvenirs of his presence have been preserved throughout the years to the present day.[67]

Six idyllic weeks went by for us until, one hot August day, Am rode triumphantly by taxi to clear off our ten pounds debt, returning lightheartedly to eat his favourite lunch of curried rabbit. We idled pleasantly at the table, talking of the new line of sweets that he had ordered until I heard the clock strike three, and thought it was time I did some work. I gathered up the dishes to wash.

"I think I'll do some gardening," said Am, and with that he picked up the mat so that he could kneel to weed.

Just then an old age pensioner came in to collect her ten shillings so he paid her, calling me to deal with her grocery order. He showed the old lady out to the gate and told her what he was going to plant in the garden next spring. I could hear him through the open window as I stood at the kitchen sink. A moment or two later I heard a boy who was passing by on his bicycle shout "Mrs. Lyth! Your husband's laid out in the garden."

With the teapot still in my hand, I ran to the door to see Am lying underneath the shop window. I heard the teapot smash at my feet and felt myself move to him. My neighbours rushed out when they heard me screaming thinking that my dog had been run over. My heart cried out "No! Please, God, no."

From the next door cottage one-armed Captain Ames[68] came running to my aid, and the landlady from the Three Horse Shoes Inn[69] rushed out with whisky for Am. They phoned for the doctor but he was not there. A strange doctor came. "He's gone," he told me gently, but I did not need to be told. My Am, my dearest Am was gone.

Some parcels came from Mr. Shaw for mailing but there was no business done that afternoon, and they had to return with them unposted. The Hon. Nall-Cain came as soon as he knew what had happened. He insisted that I should sleep at his house until after Am's funeral, all of which he arranged for me. Taking both my hands he said, "I hope we will have you here for years and years." Later he gave me a cheque to pay the funeral expenses. Both he and his wife did everything possible to ease my burden and for the kindness to me I am forever grateful. But numbed as I was I would not close down the shop. To all the requests to do so I could only reply, "Shall I feel differently in ten days, or a month?" Or, indeed, in a year or ten years? (In fact the only day the shop and post office closed was the day Am died and on the day of his funeral.)[70]

The day after his death I received the proof of the photograph of the post office. Through my tears I saw that Am too appeared on it, talking over the fence to a villager. Somehow, seeing him thus, was almost more of a shock to me than his actual death. Twenty-five years elapsed before I had the heart to sell this photograph over the counter.

The Roman Catholic priest had come to Ayot St. Lawrence to perform the last rites for my husband, there being no Catholic Church nearer than five miles. I made a little altar in my living room, then took the crucifix from over Am's bed and placed it upon his chest, and sprinkled the small bottle of Holy Water over him as he lay in his coffin. Both the crucifix and the Holy Water had been sent to us from Rome, and had been blessed by the Pope to give the grace of a happy death but, even as I wept, I knew he could not have died more happily; nor what better day to die than on August the fifteenth, the date of the Assumption of the Beloved Virgin Mary. Am went to his last resting place in the small churchyard of the New Church where we had stood and laughed together so short a time ago.

Oh, but I learned of the kindness of villagers' hearts who grieved with me, who was so newly amongst them. I wanted for nothing although I thought I wanted nothing. Mr. and Mrs. Shaw were amongst those who called to condole with me.

"I can't understand how such a fine man came to find this Godforsaken hole," said G.B.S. to me and, later, he added, "I hope I shall die like that—in the garden under the stars." (He very nearly did many years later when he fell in his garden but he, unlike my Am, had to linger a wearisome time longer before he could fall asleep forever.)

"Yes, sir," I agreed, "but not at fifty-four."

Mrs. Shaw, too, expressed her sorrow and wished me the best of luck in Ayot St. Lawrence. "We hope we'll be seeing a lot of you," she added very kindly.

In this way I was made to feel secure and wanted, and not entirely alone, and the post office agreed to let me remain as postmistress. All the kindnesses shown to me throughout the years to come stemmed, I am sure, from my tragic loss a bare six weeks after we had come to this village.

I sought comfort from my religion and seriously considered becoming a nun. Frequently I rode the five miles to Harpenden[71] on my bicycle to borrow books on theology and Catholic doctrine. I was not strong and, after I had collapsed at Mass one Sunday, the priest advised me to put away my books and carry on a normal life. The dreadful lonely days and nights dragged by.

Chapter 6

When the razor's edge of my grief had dulled a little, and I was capable of coherent thought, I realised that Am must have considered the possibility of my being left a widow and had done his best to give me some security after he had gone. He succeeded by such a narrow margin. If I had not had the post office and shop to occupy my mind and hands I do not know what would have become of me. What is there left for a woman of fifty-odd years when her husband dies, and she has no child to comfort her? There were others in the village who thought of me and tried to ease my burden, and one of these was George Bernard Shaw.

The first time he called into my shop, some weeks after Am's death, I felt nervous and shy for I knew then just how learned and world famous he was. I felt so small and insignificant that I hardly dared speak to him whilst counting out his order for stamps but, when he had gone, I realised he had in fact made me feel absolutely at my ease. From that day onwards I had no qualms and became my natural self with him.

I always attached a lot of importance to a person's voice and Mr. Shaw's was delightful. His dancing, smiling eyes of sea blue went well with his shaggy eyebrows and lilting Irish intonation, and when he laughed I liked the way his shoulders laughed too. Indeed I never saw him any other way but smiling and happy in the twenty years I knew him. At this time he was a very tall, very upright man, nearly always dressed in his well loved Norfolk suits over which his cheeky white beard jutted merrily up and down. He was never without his camera and he wore the biggest hat I have ever seen outside a cowboy film. Sometimes he sported a very long checked tweed cloak which came down to the top of his boots. Every time he came in to my shop he removed his hat, though whether out of good manners or because the cottage's low ceiling threatened to decapitate him, I never knew.

One morning when my doorbell jangled I came in to find G.B.S. jigging about impatiently at the counter.

"Would you like to have some photographs of me and my house to sell in your shop?" he asked, half bashfully, half belligerently, without so much as a "good day" to start off the conversation.

"Oh yes, *please*, sir!" I was delighted with the idea.

"I will pose with the house for you," he announced, "and bring them along when they're ready."

I had hardly time to thank him before he was gone, striding down the village and banging his walking stick energetically on the ground, leaving me gaping after him from the doorway. But after a night on it he came back clutching a large and fat envelope.

"I've been thinking about this," he started abruptly, "and I suggest you have one of me alone, and another of the house, so then you can sell two photographs instead of one." He threw the contents of the envelope on the counter.

"Choose the one you like best," commanded Mr. Shaw.

Slightly flummoxed, I looked through the bundle of photographs, every one different and all good likenesses, but there was one I plumped for right away and I paused at that. He was sitting at his desk, pen poised, ready for action.

"You've chosen Connie Ediss's.[72] It's her copyright."

"Oh dear!" I was disappointed. "What am I going to do then?" I had not got a clue about such things as copyrights.

"Nothing," G.B.S. answered with a chuckle. "She's dead and won't know anything about it!" He explained that if he had asked Connie to come to his house to take his picture the copyright was his, but as she took it with her camera and was not employed by him it was hers.

Amongst the photographs was one of him standing on a raft with only his swimming briefs on. He said an American had swum out to take it.[73]

"What could I do?" he asked me impishly, "I couldn't shoot him because I hadn't got a gun."

With that he shuffled most of them back into the envelope, leaving me another five to keep for myself, and then fished out three negatives from his wallet.

"These are of my house. I took them myself and you can have them for your postcard reproductions. No need to worry over the copyright," he added mischievously.

I tried to thank him but he would have none of it, waving away my words as he turned to go.

"Oh sir," I cried, "I've got to give it a name, haven't I?"

"Call it Shaw's Corner!" he called back over his shoulder.

And that was the first time I, at any rate, had heard his house so called.[74] It certainly needed no name for his mail to reach him. "G.B.S., England" was sufficient for that. But from that day onwards "Shaw's Corner" it was and so it became known throughout the world.

I contacted the photographer Am had employed to take the post office, and he reproduced the two photographs for me. On Shaw's negative I had him print "Shaw's Corner. Taken by G.B.S. His own photo." I had two thousand of the Connie Ediss picture to start with and sold the lot without hearing from anybody about breaking the law. Anyway I had no fears about it for had anything happened I knew Mr. Shaw would get me out of the mess! My postcards sold like the proverbial hot cakes to the Shavian pilgrims flocking to the village. There were always plenty of them about gazing wistfully through the hedges at his house in the faint hope of laying an eye on the great man himself. Hitherto no one had sold pictures of Shaw or his house, and I felt very proud that I should be the first to do so. Their sale helped to swell my tiny income which was, of course, what he had intended them to do and I was grateful to him for it. I also added half a dozen views of the village and they sold well too. I found that many of Mr. Shaw's fans came to my little store to ask where they could find his house. One day I told him this.

"I'm thinking of buying myself a camp stool, sir," I announced.

"And why, may I ask?" he replied, his eyes twinkling as he saw there was a catch in it.

"So that I can sit outside my gate and charge a halfpenny every time I am asked where you live."

"Make it two and sixpence and I'll come into business with you!" G.B.S. roared with laughter at this novel idea.

I soon got used to him coming along to drop some letters in the little post box set in the wall by my shop window, and he would chat of this and that but he was never personal in his topics of conversation. He never bought anything from the shop but I supplied all his postal requirements which he ordered regularly by letter. This was usually brought along by Mr. Day, the chauffeur,[75] when he came with Mr. Shaw's mail in time for the afternoon collection. He also sent his orders to me from his Whitehall flat for Miss Patch's needs.[76] (At that time the agile old young man of seventy-five spent half his week in London and the other half in Ayot.) How well he must have known that these big orders meant a lot to me in pepping up post office business. Once, in paying me by cheque, G.B.S. underpaid me by ten shillings; I had to send him a note pointing out his error whereupon he sent his chauffeur back post haste with a ten-shilling note, and profuse apologies.

It was not very long before it dawned on me that these missives of his were worth a darn sight more to his myriads of admirers than they were to me. So many of them asked me if I had any autograph of Mr. Shaw's for sale that I began to hoard his letters like gold to sell at ten and sixpence a time. I wondered if I would be cutting off my future supplies by telling Shaw of this but plucked up my courage to do so.

"When you're dead I'm going to sell your letters asking me for stamps," was how I put it to him.

"You'll get tuppence halfpenny for them,"[77] he mocked.

"I'm getting more than that now you're alive, sir!" I said, greatly daring.

He continued sending me his orders for the rest of his life notwithstanding.

After a time, when I saw how easily they sold, I raised the price to two guineas. As I got at least one of these letters a month this was even better in helping me along financially. G.B.S. always paid me for his stamps by cheque and, the first time he did so, he asked what name he should make his cheque out to.

"Why, Lyth, sir!" I replied, knowing full well he meant my Christian name, but I was loath to divulge that it was Jisbella for I thought he would make fun of it.

"I know that," he answered impatiently, "I want your Christian name."

"Jessie," I quibbled, which was partly true as many of my friends so called me.

But I noticed that when my name first appeared in the newspapers as postmistress of Ayot St. Lawrence he had duly remarked on the fact. The next cheque was made out to Mrs. Jisbella Lyth.

Although I never thought it of him it has sometimes been suggested that Mr. Shaw was a mean man.[78] Perhaps the village children thought so when they went to fetch their Christmas shilling from his house each year! I believe he paid for the repair of the church roof at one time, which I think was pretty generous of him considering how little time he spent in it. Maybe it was in gratitude to his first visit to Ayot when he saw the tombstone there of the lady who had died at a ripe old age; the inscription on her tombstone read "Her time was short" and that, so the story goes, convinced him that Ayot must be a good place for longevity, whereupon he decided to live there himself. Certainly he chose correctly for he beat the old lady's record by quite a few years.[79] Come to that, I am getting on a bit myself after all the Ayot St. Lawrence air I have breathed in the last twenty-seven years. Once Mr. Shaw lost his wallet. I do not know how much was in it but when two village boys found it he gave them fifty shillings reward.

As I sampled my first winter in Ayot I became aware of some of the snags. I found it bitterly cold and as there was no water laid on to my cottage I had to fetch it from a well a hundred yards off. I was so fed up with this that I was determined to mention it when next I saw Lord Brocket, my landlord.

"Would you like to see what I have to do to get a drink of water, sir?" I asked him. He nodded, somewhat surprised, so I fetched my bucket and off we went. He agreed that it was too much for me, and said he would arrange to have water laid on from his house to mine. To do this, however, meant pipes being laid under the road and the Council objected to it so, instead, Lord Brocket had the water brought as far as his own fence where he put a tap enclosed in a box to which I had the key. This was a great relief for me and I was exceedingly pleased about it. It was even better still, some years later, when I was promoted to a tap over the kitchen sink when my water supply came from the Inn which had an automatic pump. A year or so after the war the village at last got put on to the mains when a flush toilet replaced my earth closet and, what with electricity as well, life became almost modern.

I tried to fill in the long dark nights by attempting to plough through some of Shaw's words but, quite frankly, I did not understand a lot of them. Somewhat sadly I told him this whereupon he informed me I should have to read them ten times, and then I *might* have an inkling of what they were about. (Needless to say I did not read them ten times but relaxed with some lighter reading matter.) To soften this blow to my self esteem Mr. Shaw asked me if I knew that his friend Lawrence of Arabia had been in my shop the other day.[80] I was astonished for I had not been aware of the fact. "I wish he'd said who he was, sir," I replied, aggrieved to have missed such an occasion. "Never mind," was his answer, "perhaps you will [meet him] the next time he comes to see us." I never did though.

Six months had gone by since Am died and I was learning to live alone, and accepting the will of God. I still practised my religion although it was not easy cycling to Harpenden in all weathers for my Sunday Mass. At Mass one morning I collapsed and found myself in a doctor's surgery when I came round; my ribs hurt so much I thought I had broken them; electric fires were turned on full blast and hot water bottles were all around me. The priest was there too. The doctor told me I was overdoing things and must take life more easily. He took me home in his car but when he found I lived alone he was even more disturbed and did not want to leave me by myself. I had to be firm and make him go. After this I only went to Mass once a month and, when going to Holy Communion, I stayed the night previous in Harpenden so that I should not have the long, early morning, bicycle ride whilst fasting.

Then, shortly after Christmas, came a bombshell that wiped out the peace of mind I had fought so hard to gain; it came in the shape of a newspaper cutting enclosed in a letter from my brother-in-law. He wanted me to know what this was all about and, when I read it, I could not blame him for wondering at me.

The article referred to me as the happiest woman in Hertfordshire and all because of George Bernard Shaw. It described me as fondling Mr. Shaw's pictures, and of saying that he was almost my greatest friend, and that hardly a day passed but he did not come to see me, that he had been the most generous man in the world to me. I was horrified at the distorted picture this presented of me. Certainly it was true that I admired G.B.S. and was grateful to him, but to make me out a love sick woman a bare six months after my own well loved husband's death was too much for me to take. I knew instantly who was responsible for the article for, during the previous week, a taxi driver had called in to my shop, saying he had dropped "a toff" at Shaw's Corner but that he was not having much luck in getting to see G.B.S.

"The next best thing to seeing him is to see his picture," said I with an eye to business. "I sell them."

And off he went, bringing "the toff" in question a little while later. I immediately got out my postcards expecting to sell some to him. He talked to me casually and asked how I found G.B.S. I replied that I found him a kindly man and that he had sent me a Christmas box. He continued to pump me about Mr. Shaw so much that I told him I knew very little about the man, having been in Ayot such a short time. I wondered then if he was a reporter and asked him this. He acknowledged it so I sympathised with him not getting the interview he wanted with Shaw and only meeting the postmistress. "But you can leave me out of it, young man," I said to him, jokingly, whereupon he replied, "I haven't come all this way for nothing."

It never occurred to me that anything I said might be newsworthy and promptly forgot all about the incident although, now, I saw he certainly had not come to Ayot without scratching together some sort of a story for his editor. It was only then that the full horror of the implications dawned on me. *What* would Mr. Shaw think of me? Would he have seen it? Would he think it true that I had said these things? Would *Mrs.* Shaw credit it of me?

The letter arrived on my half day and I felt like using it to take my life. When my sister phoned to know how we should spend the afternoon, for we usually went out somewhere together on my free day, I could only tell her I had something to fight out and I could not come. Fight it out I did. After a ghastly night I made up my mind to write to Mr. Shaw instead of calling to see him as, being by nature an emotional person, I dared not trust my voice sufficiently to say what I wanted. I would have broken down and wept. But when he came stomping through the village next day direct to the post office, and a dismal winter's afternoon it was, his very presence gave me confidence.

"What's this about a newspaper?" he demanded, getting straight to the point.

Silently I handed him the cutting which he read by the light of my little oil lamp on the counter. He grunted once or twice as he read through it and then pointed his finger to the word "fondling."

"They should pay you £2000 for that one word, Mrs. Lyth," he said angrily, and asked me to describe the reporter to him. I did so as well as I was able.

"Give me the cutting. I'll write to the editor of that paper and put the fear of God into him." He told me I must not be upset and that it worried him not at all. "They're always thinking up something fresh about *me*," he smiled, "but I won't have them taking it out on you when they can't get to see me."

Oh the relief of his attitude to the unsavoury affair. What he wrote to the editor I do not know but, poor as I was then, I would have given £5 to have seen it. In the very next issue of the newspaper concerned an apology was printed, saying that the reporter had been over zealous in obtaining his copy. The apology was in the London edition although the original article had appeared in the provincial one. Mr. Shaw sent the paper along to me, marking the apology in blue pencil and drawing a finger pointing to it. The cutting I had given to him he returned pasted to a piece of green cardboard, and dated with the name of the newspaper in his own handwriting. This I still have.

I wrote to my brother-in-law enclosing the apology for I did not want him, of all people, to think badly of me nor that I could so soon forget my husband. Vindicated I might be by the apology but I still felt that my reputation suffered. The thought that everyone who knew me might whisper "Where there's smoke there's fire..." made me physically ill and not far off from a nervous breakdown. Thus it took a little while for Mr. Shaw's remark that they should pay for that one word alone to really penetrate, and only then did I determine they *should* pay for coupling my name, a tuppenny halfpenny postmistress, with that of a great man like Bernard Shaw.

There was an awful lot I did not know about claiming damages from a newspaper. I soon learned. It was like knocking my head against a brick wall and trying to get blood out of a stone all at the same time. I put my case in the hands of a solicitor, who wrote to the newspaper concerned only to be informed that they did not consider the article to be defamatory in any way. This was despite the fact that they had printed an apology. Indeed even my solicitors advised me that the apology could wash out my case but to this I replied that it was Mr. Shaw, not I, who had asked for it. I instructed them to carry on for I can be pretty determined when I get going. In answer to this I received an offer of fifteen guineas and my solicitors' costs to settle the matter, although they still insisted that the article was not defamatory to me in any way. This I turned down as being utterly ridiculous, which attitude seemed to pay dividends for the offer was then raised to £30 and costs although still insisting I had not got a case against them. I had the sense to refuse this offer too which was just as well for, a week later, it had gone up to £50 and costs, plus an intimation that they would go no higher and if I did not take it they would institute proceedings.

Presumably they expected me to agree to this but my dander was by then well and truly up, and I did not care a fig whether they took proceedings or not for, in my estimation, they had already admitted to being in the wrong by making me an offer at all. I said that I would accept £100 and costs and not a penny less. A month later I had their cheque in payment for agreed damages of £100 and my solicitor's costs.

When I told Mr. Shaw how much I had got he was very angry and said I should have asked for more. However, three months of not knowing whether or not I would end up in court, coupled with the thought of dragging poor G.B.S. into it, had left me a bit of a nervous wreck as it was and I was glad to call it day for I now had undeniable proof of my innocence. Poor fool that I was, had I carried on I might have had a nice fat bank balance today but, in those pre-war days, even £100 meant a small fortune to me. I had never before seen that much money never mind possessing it.

Strangely enough reactions to the incident in the village were precisely nil as far as I could gather. Certainly no one ever remarked upon it to me. Of course my sister and my friends were on tenterhooks with me and very much relieved when it was all over. With the money I bought Snow a new costume, a savings certificate for £60 for myself, plus a new bicycle and a very smart black and white checked coat with a velvet collar. I began to feel a lot better, but one result of the episode was that I was half afraid to speak to Mr. Shaw at all in case someone should try to make something of it, and it entirely spoiled the friendly relationship we had enjoyed for some considerable time. Nor did G.B.S. set foot in my shop for a very long time although his stamp orders were sent to me as regularly as before but, should we meet whilst out walking in the village, he would always stop for a chat, and would talk awhile with me over my fence when he came to post his mail.

I did an awful lot of walking in my free time which did my health good and, in the beautiful serenity of the countryside, I regained my peace of mind. I had my dogs to thank for getting me out and about. Lady was getting on now and I had been given another puppy, a mongrel of course, whom I called Nada and it did not take her long to enlarge my doggy family to three; that one I named Tess. I was often called The Lady with the Three Dogs by strangers in the village. Mr. Shaw always had a kind word for them when he met us and often asked me if I made myself a slave to them. I am afraid I did.

When I asked him about his own dog he replied, "He's lying in the kitchen too fat to move because he gets six meals a day!" During the war when he asked if my dogs were vegetarians I could only answer "Hobson's choice, sir."[81] When Lady died Nada produced yet another puppy as if to compensate me. That's right, another girl, so I christened her Ladybird.

One lovely spring day a gentleman came into the shop to ask if I would give him a meal. I pointed out that the Inn next door would serve him [but] he said he did not like eating in pubs. Just to oblige him, I boiled an egg and gave him this with some bread and butter for his tea. He appeared to be pleased with such simple fare. "Why don't you serve teas all the time?" was his question as he left. And why, I thought, don't I?

It did not enter my head to seek permission from anyone before transforming my premises into a tea garden. Nowadays I suppose I should have countless forms to complete and Heaven knows what else and then, more than likely, such a thing would not be allowed. I just bought some outdoor tables and chairs out of what was left of my hundred pounds capital, erected a shelter in my tiny garden, and turned the two upstairs rooms into tea rooms after moving my bed downstairs to the living room. Then I hoisted a board outside announcing the fact that I was in business and, the first weekend I opened, I was run off my feet with custom.

Fortunately, the majority of my trade was at week-ends. Otherwise I could not have managed shop, post office, and tea all at once. Whether it was the quaintness of the cottage, the lure of Ayot's isolation, the fact that London was but twenty-five miles away, or my simple fare I do not know but, once a customer always a customer, proved to be a true maxim for me. By the following summer I was so well established that I had to hire a woman to help me *and* I could afford to do so. Instead of just buttering my bread the modest tea rooms put just a little jam on it as well.

Quite a few of my restaurant customers still come to see me but they say I have spoilt the atmosphere of this five-hundred-years-old cottage by having electricity installed. They liked it best sitting before a log fire with a sixty-candle power lamp hanging from the ceiling. The hook is still there from which it hung and many people today ask me what it is for. The best answer I can think of is that [it] is there ready for me when I am tired of living!

Chapter 7

Although there were tourists who came to Ayot purely because of its old world charm, and some who fell upon it accidentally whilst exploring the beckoning country lanes leading off from the main London road, some three odd miles away, the majority came because of G.B.S. So, again in an indirect fashion, I had Mr. Shaw to thank that my tea gardens not only continued to prosper but that there was again some purpose in life for me. No longer did I have time to feel lonely or sorry for myself for, even in the dead of winter, someone always lingered in my little upstairs room with the sloping, beamed ceiling as they sipped hot tea and hugged the fire. They came from all over the world and, if only to prove true the saying what a small world it is, I mention the two ladies who admired my collection of Chinese brasses.

"I was several years in China," I explained.

"*I* was twenty-seven years there," laughed one. Of course there was then much nostalgic talk between us of our respective days in Hong Kong, but I did not expect to discover that both she and I had, at different times, lived in *the very same house* there.

I might have had Shaw to thank for my custom but there were times, too, when I reached the point of never wanting to hear his name mentioned again. It was G.B.S. this, or Bernard Shaw that, around my tea tables until I could have screamed. And the questions fired at me on the same subject followed such a stereotyped pattern that, at times, I could hardly be bothered to answer except that one must always be polite to the customer.

"Do you ever see Mr. Shaw?" usually came first.

"Oh, yes, quite often."

Sighs of envy and awe followed my casual reply, usually combined with ejaculations ranging from an English "By Jove!" to an American "Well, what d'ya know?"

"Does he post his letters *here* in your little post office?"

"Oh, yes, indeed he does. It's the only post box in the village."

More cries of astonishment and then, with hope-brightened faces, "Do you think he might come along *this afternoon*?"

"Oh yes, it's quite possible but," I would add pessimistically, "I wouldn't count on it if I were you."

"Do you think G.B.S. would see us if we called on him?" some were brash enough to ask although, admittedly, many who enquired thus were writers, journalists, or photographers.

"There are only two answers you can get from Mr. Shaw, yes and no," was my stock reply to this one, "and you'll get one of them!"

On the occasions when Mr. Shaw did stride along to push his mail into the little post box, the craning of heads and the excited whisperings made me chuckle. The object of all the attention seemed quite oblivious although, of course, he was perfectly well aware of it. He would always pose for his photograph but, never, never, never would he sign an autograph. Mrs. Shaw, should she be with him, would promptly vanish the moment a camera was produced; she just hated the sight of them and would not be photographed for love or money. There were times when I was able to browbeat Mr. Shaw into meeting an admirer only, I might add, if I thought that said admirer might appeal to him in any way.

One such, a young solicitor, was a fervent Shavian who visited my tea garden frequently, and he and I became good friends. He brought two exercise books bulging with Shaw cuttings for me to see one afternoon and, as it so happened, G.B.S. came by and paused to chat when he had posted his letters. I showed him the exercise books and asked if he would care to meet the ardent collector. He allowed me to introduce my young friend, Mr. Currall,[82] but wasted no time in pointing out that collecting newspaper cuttings was in his opinion, a complete waste of time. The two men got along well together notwithstanding and, out of this meeting, a lasting friendship grew between them; but, undeterred by Shaw's advice, Mr. Currall continued to amass Shaw cuttings and, today, possesses a singular collection of them and is able to answer G.B.S. queries whatever part of the globe they come from. It was through Ivo Currall and myself that Dr. Loewenstein[83] became Mr. Shaw's bibliographer, but more of that later.

Another young man whom I befriended, Ted Orme,[84] had two passions—cycling, by which he discovered Ayot St. Lawrence in the first place, and photography. He begged me to ask Mr. Shaw to allow him to take his photograph and this I managed to arrange quite easily. As Shaw had already posted his letters that day I produced an old envelope for him, and he posed holding this poised at the mouth of the post box while Ted clicked his camera. Ted also took a second shot of Mr. Shaw paying me for some stamps which, by the way, was the only cash transaction there ever was between us; it was completely candid camera work for neither Mr. Shaw nor I knew we had been taken. When the photographs were developed we were delighted with the results; both were beauties and both have been published many times since. I know I am no Gladys Cooper[85] but, oh dear! G.B.S. of course, came out his usual photogenic self.

In Ayot we do our share of collecting for various charities, and when it was my turn to go around with the collection box for the hospitals Shaw's Corner was included on my calling list. The maid answered the door and said she would ask Mr. Shaw if he would donate a little something but, to my surprise, she came back saying that G.B.S. wished to see me in the drawing room. He proceeded to read me a lecture.

"Hospitals should not have to beg," Mr. Shaw concluded with some asperity, "they should be run and kept up by the State."[86]

"They would be called infirmaries, or unions, or some other ghastly name then, sir," I replied feelingly, "and no one would go into them. They'd look upon it as a charity, like the workhouse."

"Not if everybody had to use them!" he insisted, and rattled on with lots more far above my poor intelligence.

This was in 1933 and I had no idea that, one day, things would be just as he said; now, under our National Health Scheme, anybody and everybody can have the same treatment in all the hospitals, free. Then, however, I had given up hope of adding to my collection from him and prepared to leave. He followed me to the door, opened it, and let me out saying, "I am not grumbling at you, Mrs. Lyth, but they always seem to hit on the parson's wife or someone in an official position, like yourself, to do the dirty work." After all that he pushed a folded pound note into my box.

The first inkling I had of being "immortalised" by Shaw was when Mr. Currall called by. "When did Mr. Shaw see *you* wooing?" he enquired, laughing. Nonplussed, I asked him to explain what he meant; he told me there was a new short play of Shaw's running in London called *Village Wooing*.[87] I must have been pretty busy, or else I was not paying too much attention, for I attached little importance to his account of it, and never thought another thing about this new play of Shaw's until, carrying my tea tray upstairs to serve a lady with her son and daughter, I heard them discussing *Village Wooing*. As I set out the tea I asked if they could tell me more about it. This the lady could, and did, adding that it was her husband, Arthur Wontner, and Sybil Thorndike who were playing the two parts in it at the Little Theatre.[88] "Do you know," she smiled, "we were wondering if you were the lady who inspired the play?"

Scenes from *Village Wooing*, Little Theatre, 1934 (Mander and Mitchenson 233)

This took me aback considerably, especially as I was about to remark that it sounded jolly monotonous, so I hastily agreed when she said I really ought to see it for myself. By now I was just about bursting with curiosity, and the following week saw me in London watching myself through Shaw's eyes, for if the character was not based on me, my name was not Jisbella either. It was a peculiar and somewhat uncomfortable experience, and not in the least flattering, but I had to acknowledge that he had got me down to the last "Thank you very much." Whilst admitting that I am inclined to be a trifle garrulous by nature I fervently hoped that "Z," my stage self, was an exaggerated version of me.

Sybil Thorndike acted the part of a village postmistress so wonderfully that I felt she could take over my life in reality any day of the week. I wrote to tell her so and she replied, with an autographed photograph, saying, "Interested to learn that I have been playing you! Thank you so much for your letter—I shall come to see you one day." Both she and Arthur Wontner autographed a photograph of my real life post office for me but, to my great disappointment, Sybil Thorndike never did come to Ayot after all. *Village Wooing* being but a one-act play was followed by Galsworthy's *Little Man*[89] and, let me whisper it, this I enjoyed a darn sight better, probably because it had nothing at all to do with me.

Incidentally, the part of "A" played by Arthur Wontner was to me, if no one else, none other than G.B.S. If "A's" beard had been white instead of black, then it was the great man himself, tall, graceful, and lissom; it was not only his appearance that gave me this impression—the lines he spoke smacked very much of Mr. Shaw although he was never so rude to me as he was to poor "Z," thank goodness. In later years, upon learning from Miss Patch's book that Shaw had written *Village Wooing* whilst nearing China on his World Tour,[90] it seemed more than co-incidental that I should have crept into his mind for he well knew I had lived in Hong Kong for some time.

I had not seen a lot of G.B.S. prior to investigating *Village Wooing* for myself; he seemed to be perpetually touring some part of the world or other around the time but, on the occasions I had talked with him, he never uttered one word about putting me into any play of his. I waited a long time before plucking up enough courage to ask him if I *was* the woman in it. An arch "Ah!" was all I got for an answer leaving me, I supposed, to draw my own conclusions. Nothing more was ever said on the subject in all the years that followed.

The day after I had seen the play I was, naturally, dying to talk about it to anyone who came into the shop, and when a sympathetic gentleman called in he bore the full brunt of my enthusiasm, positively bowing to me as I announced proudly "I am in it!" In those days I could never differentiate between a newspaper man and any other, although I most certainly can now, and this particular male subsequently turned out to be the editor of a county newspaper. Again, all innocence, I did not connect his visit with a phone call from a photographer asking if he might take my picture for someone who wanted it. When I asked him "Who?" he said he did not know, which struck me as being so idiotic that I consented, and posed for him at the gate with one of my dogs. I was genuinely surprised then when my sister phoned me, full of excitement, about the wonderful article in the *Hert[fordshire] Mercury*,[91] with me and my connection with *Village Wooing* as the subject matter. I demanded her to read her copy of it forthwith as Ayot, being Ayot, I had not a hope of seeing it otherwise. To my great relief the article drew a charming picture of me, and anything it quoted me as saying I had, in fact, said; the photograph also amazed me by being a fairly reasonable likeness for once.

Nevertheless, bearing in mind my last appearance in print, in connection with Mr. Shaw, I was faintly alarmed to think what he might say when he heard of my claim to be the inspiration of *Village Wooing*. I took the devil by the tail and wrote to G.B.S., who was then in Malvern,[92] enclosing a copy of the article and telling him that, although true, I had not been aware my words were going to be published, and enquiring if *his* permission had been sought. He sent me a letter card bearing a picture of the Malvern Hotel at which he was staying; his first words on it were, "Never mind; the newspapers always improve a story; and this one will do the village no harm." He added, "I am quite sure you are as innocent of the affair as I am myself." How glad I was to read it and, as he had not contradicted my claim to being the postmistress of his play, I felt reasonably certain that I was.

Fully aware then of the great honour of being immortalised I was a little surprised that none of the villagers so much as remarked upon it to me; of course, my tragedy was still very fresh in everybody's minds and also, no doubt, I was still regarded as a "foreigner." Even Shaw once said that he was regarded as an interloper in Ayot for fourteen years. One gentleman did tell me I ought to be proud to have G.B.S. as a friend and, of course, I was proud to think so. My own folks, particularly Snow, were very excited over the whole thing but, would you believe it, not one of them ever went to see *Village Wooing* performed!

After this I stopped being surprised at finding myself featuring in the news from time to time in anything from the post office magazine to the *Hyderabad Bulletin*. Although I tried not to get big headed, telling myself firmly it was merely reflected glory, it was very difficult not to do so but I think I succeeded. Several visitors to the village remarked on my popularity with Mr. Shaw and said, "Now we have seen you we know why." I modestly stated that anyone could be like me. "No," they insisted, "you have a very charming personality." I do not like repeating this flattery but if I am to tell my story I must record it. However, I do feel that G.B.S. liked me because I did not pester him or unduly worry him in any way.

The London *Tatler*[93] devoted its central pages to G.B.S., myself, and Ayot and, under my photograph, appeared the words "Mrs. Jisbella Lyth, Postmistress, second only in importance to G.B.S." However, the text went on to say, "There are only three main sights—G.B.S., the village postmistress, Mrs. Jisbella Lyth, and the old village church." I felt rather like an ancient monument! A London newspaper put me down as being the most remarkable character in the village next to Shaw so, somehow or other, the names Jisbella, G.B.S., and Ayot always seemed to go together. It was surprising, too, the extraordinary bits of information that crept into these articles; one item stated that, on average, there is one dog per fifteen people in Britain but that, in Ayot, there were ninety-three inhabitants and eighty dogs and, what's more, three of them were in my kitchen! Not even the wasps that forever buzzed about at my tea garden went unrecorded. To a man busily swotting at them I am quoted as saying, "You're not to kill the wasps. They're my babies." As well as all this I found that many newspapers, including the *New York Times*, were only too glad to pay me a couple of guineas a time for the loan of my negatives of Shaw's Corner.

The next great excitement was when electric light came to the village. I was the first to have it installed, and when Mr. Shaw came into the shop I switched it on very ostentatiously. "You see, sir, I've got the light!"

"Yes," he answered, "and do you know what follows the light?"

"No, sir."

"Buildings," he answered gloomily.

I knew he would not like his house built around and said so.

"Don't you realise it's the public that keeps you and me?" he replied to that resignedly.

However, the coming of electricity to Ayot brought me an electric cooker and an urn, both of which proved a boon to me in serving teas; also the urn heated my weekly bath water very satisfactorily! But there was still no street light in Ayot and this is still a bone of contention today. Just prior to acquiring electricity I read a letter in my daily paper from someone living one hundred miles from London; it said that in their village they had no light, doctor, nurse, or school but that they did get their *Daily* -------- delivered.[94] I could not let this pass without writing a reply that, although *only twenty-five* miles from London, we had none of the facilities mentioned *and* we had no newspaper delivery. *We* had to rely upon the courtesy of the butcher, the baker, or the candlestick maker to bring our daily paper. This brought a representative of the *Daily* -------- to see me to know why we did not get our papers delivered. He went to all the surrounding villages within a radius of five miles to see if he could work the oracle for us. He got the same reply. It would not pay them to include Ayot St. Lawrence on its round—too few inhabitants and too out of the way.

When the second world war broke out[95] little Ayot tried to do its bit too. We had a searchlight battery stationed about a mile from the village and, when the team searched the night sky for enemy planes on their way to London, we really felt part of the war effort; we had a siren that went off each night at six o'clock like clockwork, not that we ever did anything particular about it. We did have a landmine drop near the searchlight battery but it did no damage except to break a few windows and bring down the ceiling plaster of the farm nearby. Eight small bombs fell another night but, fortunately, only in various gardens and open fields. We had one doodle bug, the noise of which frightened us more than the actual explosion, and which blew in one of Shaw's windows.[96] De Havillands took over Ayot House to accommodate their staff, a bus taking them to their offices in Hatfield each day.[97] Later on in the war the Land Army girls replaced them and a grand lot of girls they were.[98] I had two of the overflow billeted with me for a time; they still write to let me know how many children are in their family and, in general, keep me up to date.

The blackout caused more inconvenience than the bombs. I switched my light off and on one night, just for a second, to speed a parting guest at the precise moment a police car came around the corner. "Who put that light on?" Well, who else but Jisbella? They knew. I was given a stern warning but, the night the bombs were dropping around midnight, I flashed my light once again to get the geography of my twisty stairway. Our one and only warden was outside. "Put that light out!" he yelled.

Tartly I shouted back, "I'd rather pay a £5 fine than break my leg."

"That's a real Shavian answer," he replied with a chuckle, so I got away with it.

When I was asked to take in evacuees I refused, saying I preferred to choose my own, and so I began to take in paying guests. My first, a married couple with a young child, stayed with me for two years and a tight squeeze it was in my little cottage, but it was nothing to what followed during the worst of London's blitz. Then I was inundated with requests for beds for a night, two nights, or a week's rest from the incessant bombing which we, in Ayot, could hear and see for all our isolation, and grief was in our hearts. I put them all up somehow, regardless of lack of space; they slept on makeshift beds, tables, mattresses on the floor and under the stairs. At one point, one of my sisters brought herself and her family from Southampton to seek relief from the raids. Somehow, seven of us and three dogs managed to live together in that confined space for several months.

The rationing soon did away with my tea business;[99] it was no longer possible to cope with the unexpected guests unless they brought their own food, or emergency ration cards, and that is what most of my lodgers had to do. The shop soon went the same way for I just could not contend with coupons and such like palaver, it was too much of a headache. Personally, I was not badly off for food; I received a lot of food parcels from American friends (but for Shaw, I would not have met them) and how welcome they were. I also got soap, tins of meat, and other useful items of which we were short, from Australia. These latter things came through the Council to be distributed to widows who lived alone. I slept downstairs now as a matter of habit and never went back to using the upstairs bedroom even after the war.

I only had reason to travel once during the war, to a niece's wedding, in West Hartlepool. The train was packed with troops and I, of course, a mere civilian, had no priority whatever. I got stuck in the corridor and spent a lot of the long journey with my head supported by an R.A.F. officer's shoulder while I snoozed on my feet. Some of the men came from such isolated stations that they humorously requested me to let them know when the war was over.

I trained as a V.A.D.[100] but never had any reason to use my new-found knowledge except during the odd Home Guard manoeuvre and then it was more of a lark than anything else.[101] I also ran Whist Drives in aid of the Red Cross in the Village Hall, and one or two in Ayot House with the Land Army's permission. Towards the end of the war, at a Village Fête, I entered the Fancy Dress as a Land Girl, breeches and all, sixty-odd years old though I was. I was expecting two new gentlemen guests that same afternoon and was on the look out for them so, when I saw two strangers, I was convinced these were they. "Excuse me. Are you Mr. S....." I queried. "No," said one, giving me a naughty look, "but I wish I was!" I left them hurriedly at that but I did get a prize at the fête. At another fête I dressed as a Court lady of the past, having hired a special costume from a Court dressmaker. I walked away with the First Prize which was soap, a great luxury at that time, it might have been gold I was so pleased with it. I nipped home to change into a more suitable dress for serving at my stall only to find I could not get myself out of my costume, and I was reduced to calling in a total stranger from the street to help me out of it.

In the lighter spring and summer evenings, when blackout problems did not exist, it was a real pleasure to walk out with my dogs, and it was on one of these rambles that I met G.B.S. with another gentleman, a stranger to me.

They stopped and I was introduced to Gabriel Pascal[102] who, hearing that I was the postmistress of Ayot, told me of a youthful escapade with another charming postmistress in his native country. Mr. Shaw chuckled, his old shoulders heaving, and I retired much confused to finish my walk.

Esmé Percy, President of the Shaw Society and who acted in many of Shaw's plays,[103] dropped in to buy pictures of Shaw and Shaw's Corner one day, and talked to my three mongrels lovingly. He made a striking impression on me for he was wearing a straw hat although it was the middle of winter. I met him many times again and for the last time, although I did not know it then, at the re-opening of Shaw's Corner in April 1957. I was distressed to read of his sudden death a month or two later.

It was during the war, too, that Yousuf Karsh of Ottawa[104] came and photographed G.B.S. Mr. Shaw, knowing I had almost exhausted my stocks of the original picture he had given me, called to show me the fourteen studies Karsh had taken of him telling me to look through them at my leisure and choose whichever one I liked. He would then ask Karsh's permission for me to sell them. I realised this would be a wonderful scoop for me and dithered about which to pick. I sent them to Mr. Currall to ask his advice on the matter and then, to my great dismay, Mr. Shaw called back the very next day to collect them. I very apologetically explained what I had done. "Never mind," he told me, adding that he would be in London for the rest of the week. I promised I would phone Mr. Currall and ask him to put the photographs in the mail direct to him at Whitehall. This was done so I had to wait until G.B.S. returned to Ayot to see them again. I told him my choice.

"How many do you want, a thousand?" he asked.

"Yes, please," I almost shouted.

He arranged with Karsh that I could sell them, paying only reproduction fees on the photographs. I had no trouble selling these postcards but when the first thousand had gone Mr. Shaw was on his death bed and, without his hand to help me, I was unable to get a further supply.

The war ended[105] and, although we had not suffered unduly, that did not stop us feeling the untold relief of peace regained. A crowd of us went to Wheathampstead to rejoice, Mrs. Laden[106] and Dr. Loewenstein amongst us; the streets were floodlit and people were dancing to any old thing that would rattle out a tune; the men were smothered in lipstick from kissing all and sundry but our joy was tempered with sadness, for three boys would never return. Our local war hero was the son of one of my "evacuees." He had been a sailor on the *Prince of Wales*[107] and spent over three years as a prisoner of the Japanese. When he got home we fêted him and hung the village with banners of welcome.

CHAPTER 8

On a bright July afternoon in 1943 Mr. Currall phoned me to beg a favour. A Dr. Loewenstein, he told me, who had founded the Shaw Society,[108] and his daughter were already on their way out to Ayot St. Lawrence to call upon Mr. Shaw, being desperately keen to meet the great man face to face. Suggesting that they come to see me first, Mr. Currall put them on a bus to Kimpton (a village two-and-a-half miles from Ayot), and now asked me if I would be on the lookout for them and shepherd them on to Shaw's Corner. Spotting strangers in Ayot presents no problem so I soon had them ensconced in my cottage sipping cups of tea to refresh them after their long walk.

Dr. Loewenstein, now that he had got so far as Ayot, suddenly developed cold feet about bearding the lion in his den, and was calling the venture off but I told him he must not be so silly, that I was sure Mr. Shaw would see him if he went along. "I'll phone him then," I said as he still shrank from thrusting himself forward uninvited. Maggie, the parlourmaid, answered the phone, so I asked her to see if Mr. Shaw would meet Dr. Loewenstein, explaining who he was; she was very soon back to say that G.B.S. would be available in twenty minutes. This news settled the cold feet although the poor man still looked quite pale with anticipation, and I saw himself and his daughter safely through Shaw's gate in time for their appointment. The meeting that followed was recorded by him in my visitors' book: "F.E. Loewenstein was recommended by Ivo Currall to Mrs. Lyth, who made an appointment with G.B.S. on July 7th, 1943. This led in due course to his appointment as Shaw's Bibliographer and Remembrancer."

It was only after they had gone into the house that I noticed it was already past four-thirty; I remembered they hoped to catch the last bus from Kimpton at seven o'clock as they were dining with Mr. and Mrs. Currall before returning to London. As it is a tidy walk to Kimpton I began to get worried when they still had not appeared at half past six. However, a minute or two later, the Loewensteins deep in conversation with G.B.S. arrived on my doorstep. I told them they would miss their bus unless they looked slippy and took a short cut through the woods. "I will show you the way," I offered.

"I'll show them," Mr. Shaw announced, "I've been to Kimpton many times," so they bade me farewell and set off at a smart pace.

Half an hour later they were back again as large as life, G.B.S. looking sheepish. "They've been cutting the trees down and I couldn't find the path," he excused himself.

He told the Loewensteins to bed down in the Inn for the night and he would foot the bill; they thanked him and said goodbye, but when he had left us, they asked me if it was possible to get a taxi to Luton.[109] I ordered them one from Welwyn and went along for the ride as the taxi would be returning the same way but, when Mrs. Currall saw me, she insisted that I stay to dinner too. I enjoyed a wonderful meal, not at all spoiled by being kept waiting, but I noticed that Dr. Loewenstein did not eat a bite; he was far too elated by his meeting with Mr. Shaw to take any interest in food.

The discussion as to whether or not he would become Shaw's official bibliographer was still going on weeks later when G.B.S., Dr. Loewenstein, and Mr. Currall stopped outside my gate. I was busy with my teas and paid little attention to them so I was astonished, on going upstairs some minutes afterwards, to find Mr. Shaw being given a conducted tour of my cottage by Mr. Currall. G.B.S. never having been further than the shop was surprised to find just how attractive I had made my small domain. "What a lovely old house you have, Mrs. Lyth," he remarked almost enviously.

Mr. and Mrs. Shaw moved to their London flat to spend a few weeks there in order to relieve the small staff at Shaw's Corner and Mrs. Shaw, being so very poorly, had been needing day and night attention for some time past, and Mrs. Higgs, the housekeeper,[110] was not so well as she might have been either. It seemed a very short while after they had gone that I heard the news of Mrs. Shaw's death[111] on the radio and, when G.B.S. returned to Ayot alone some time later, he brought me about fifty postcard photographs of her, which he had taken, and gave them to [me] saying that I could sell them.

"Why, sir," I exclaimed in surprise, "Mrs. Shaw didn't like publicity. She wouldn't like this."

"She won't know anything about it," he whispered, putting his finger to his lips.

I am afraid my skin went rather goosey hearing him speak so lightly of her, but I realised later she had suffered a lot and her death was a happy release. Her photographs sold well, although I told him he should have chosen a pretty background for her and not those old steps; he had plenty of pretty spots to choose from in his garden; my favourite part was what he called The Dell.

When Mr. Shaw said he proposed giving me a book for my Christmas box I tried to look suitably pleased but I had some misgivings. My intuition proved correct. It was a copy of *Everybody's Political What's What?*![112] "Sleepy reading for Xmas" was inscribed on the fly leaf in his own unmistakable hand. It did not send me to sleep for the simple reason I could not bring myself to attempt the struggle of ploughing through it. I thanked him but could not refrain from saying the book was beyond me. He pointed out, as he had done once before, that I would have to read it ten times before I could understand it; even twenty, I thought to myself, would not do the trick but, in all seriousness, I knew that an autographed copy of any of his writings was a gift to be valued. It has since vanished from my possession, but then I have only myself to blame for leaving it lying about when I always had so many strangers in and out of my shop.

Another time Miss Patch brought me along a copy of *Pygmalion* saying that Mr. Shaw had sent this to a good girl. When I opened it I found he had inscribed it, as she said, "To a good girl."[113] I did read this one and was a trifle surprised to find I could enjoy and understand it. In a fit of misguided generosity I later auctioned this copy in aid of a local charity but, to my lasting disgust, it fetched only two guineas so that was another total loss. However, I still have and cherish *A Black Girl in Search of God*[114] and an omnibus edition of *The Complete Plays of Bernard Shaw*,[115] which includes *Village Wooing*. These two I bought myself and, breaking my rule, asked Mr. Shaw to autograph them for me. Instead of doing so then and there on the counter as I expected he carried them back to his house, although the omnibus alone was no light weight for a fragile old man to carry. He duly brought them back having written "To my good friend and neighbor, Mrs. Jisbella Lyth." In *The Black Girl* and in the omnibus, he autographed his frontispiece photograph to me.

When the film of *Caesar and Cleopatra* was showing in London Mr. Shaw sent me a message via Mrs. Laden, asking if I would like to join his domestic staff whom he was sending to London in his car to see it, tickets provided. I was having a nasty attack of fibrositis and had to get permission from my doctor to go; he agreed, providing I took a hot water bottle for my back! After all these preliminaries I did not enjoy the film much although the fibrositis might have had something to do with it. Shaw sent me two seats for *The Doctor's Dilemma* on another occasion in which Vivien Leigh acted.[116]

I was friendly with Mrs. Laden and often visited her quarters in Shaw's Corner to play bridge; we were both very keen players. Indeed, on one occasion, we finished so late that I stayed the night on a mattress on the floor. Mrs. Laden always waited until Shaw's bathwater had run out, and his bedroom door closed, before she would go to bed herself.

G.B.S. was an enormous help to me with my crossword puzzles. I loved to do the one in the *Daily Telegraph* but frequently got stuck in it,[117] and I cheated by waylaying Mr. Shaw when he came to the post. He invariably knew the answer before I had finished reading out the clue to him. Nowadays that poor old crossword rarely gets finished by me. Sometimes I would wonder why he bothered with me at all for he did not have much to say to others in the village, and the occasions he actively participated in any of the village activities could be counted on one hand.

Once he was wheedled into giving a talk to our Women's Institute.[118] As soon as I heard this startling news I made a bet with a friend that quarrelling would be the subject of his talk, *and* I won my bet but only I knew that a day or two before I had asked G.B.S. why people quarrelled so much locally. "Because they've nothing else to think about," was his reply. I suppose he was right at that. I asked him if I might invite Mrs. Currall along to hear him. He immediately agreed, telling me to send her along to his house and that he would take her himself. At the meeting he told us that if we had to quarrel we might as well do it the right way. Boiled down it amounted to this: an imaginary Mrs. Brown should get up and tell a likewise Mrs. Jones what she thought of her, then Mrs. Jones could retaliate in like fashion. After that the air should have cleared between them and they could go and have a friendly cup of tea together. He, himself, never took tea and left the meeting as soon as he finished talking.

There was, at one time, a Boys' Club of sorts which met in the tiny village hall, and in this Shaw took some slight interest. Once he actually attended one of their meetings. As he arrived he found a few of the lads disporting themselves on the handkerchief lawn outside. "What's this, a revolution?" G.B.S. barked and, striding into the hall, proceeded to enjoy himself hugely. The then adjoining neighbours complained of the noise, quite justifiably in my estimation, whereupon they rudely told them: "We were here before you. We aren't going away. You took that cottage with your eyes open, and what I advise you to do is to take a cottage next door to a farm."

He attended an organ recital in the New Church, at which John Hunt, the talented musician, his mother, and Beryl Ireland combined to give a charming performance. (Mr. Hunt's mother often came to sit in my room to write poetry; she said the atmosphere inspired her.) I had engaged a photographer to take some pictures of this occasion as a village keepsake and, when the recital was over, I asked Mr. Shaw if he would pose with the Rector and the musicians before the light went from the church steps.

"No peace on a Sunday, Mrs. Lyth?" he grumbled at me in an injured fashion.

"No, sir, not even on a Sunday," said I firmly.

He did pose, of course, and very nicely too although it was too late to catch the light with the church as a background; instead the tombstones peeped between them rather coyly.[119]

When G.B.S. really came to the fore, and surpassed himself in Ayot's estimation, was at the installation of a memorial gate at the entrance to the churchyard of the ruined church. This would have to happen when I was in hospital but I got a first hand account of the ceremony from the Rector when he came to visit me. He told me Shaw spoke as well as ever he had heard a Bishop speak![120] This wrought iron gateway looks light as a feather so daintily is it designed, its lines worked into the form of angels and birds, and was designed by Mrs. Winsten,[121] the sculptress and artist, who also lived in Ayot at that time across the road from Shaw's Corner. This same lady was responsible for the statue of St. Joan in Shaw's garden, and to which Mr. Shaw was very much attached. The first time I saw it I was disappointed to find, not a young girl as I had imagined, but an older, eagle faced woman, shading her eyes with one hand and gazing towards her birthplace as I believe a compass bearing was taken to get this right. The Old Ruins churchyard is kept as a garden, as are the flower beds and lawn outside it, in memory of those who fell in the two wars. All the work entailed is done voluntarily by those who live in Ayot.

Came Mr. Shaw's 90th birthday and all the village trooped down to his house to sing "Happy birthday to you," but their breaths were wasted for he was in London that day. Wily as ever, he had thought to avoid the usual birthday influx of newspaper reporters and cameramen by this ruse. Mr. Day, his chauffeur, had passed me the word so I was not amongst the well wishers, but when I met him out walking with a neighbour the next day I said, "I didn't come to wish you many happy returns of the day, sir, but I will when you're a hundred."

"God forbid!" he piously replied, jerking his stick up in salute.

As time went on his height seemed to diminish, and he became more and more ethereal looking although he still strode the country lanes quite vigorously, and his camera still went with him. He asked me to stand at my gate one day as he wanted to take my photograph; I posed very obligingly but for all that I never saw the result of it![122] He was not the only one to make this request for there were innumerable people with cameras at the ready, many of them journalists and writers, and many is the time I have popped upstairs so that they could take a shot of the post office with me looking through the window. Usually they would send me a copy of the photograph or article that resulted from their trip to Ayot. Sometimes I was able to help them achieve a meeting with Mr. Shaw, particularly if I took a fancy to them myself.

One young American girl from Vassar College,[123] whose ambition it was to be a writer and an actress, was so determined to meet G.B.S. that she tried every known method. I advised her as to what I thought was the best procedure. That girl did see him by the simple method of walking in and surprising him at his desk. Her subsequent article of the meeting appeared in *Life* magazine. She sent me a copy of it and a food parcel for Christmas.[124] A young man wrote to thank me for arranging for him to see the statue of St. Joan and finished, "I suppose the next best thing to interviewing G.B.S. himself, is to be able to talk to the celebrated postmistress of Ayot St. Lawrence! What would the sage say to that?" I wonder indeed. Another ardent admirer of Shaw, with whom I became friends, wrote, "I managed to kiss his hand twice." Yet all this adulation seemed almost strange to me who knew Mr. Shaw only as the grand old man of the village, who was my very good friend.

He strolled into my office one day and demanded to be shown the Electoral Roll. I handed it to him wondering what on earth he wanted with it.

"I've just been given the Freedom of Dublin," he grinned at me mischievously, "and I want to see if I'm on the Electoral Roll because now I don't know if I am an Englishman or an Irishman."[125]

Another visit he made was more interesting to me. "I'm thinking of compiling a little guide to Ayot St. Lawrence for you to sell to the people who come to the village," he announced. "Do you think it would sell, Mrs. Lyth?"[126]

I thanked him saying, "*Anything* by you, sir, would sell." This could never have been put better I afterwards realised! But I was thrilled at the prospect of being the sole vendor of one of Shaw's works, even a minor one of this sort, which proved to be his last; I knew full well it would sell like hot cakes and would do a lot to increase my income. He went off well pleased with my enthusiastic reception of his idea.

I saw him at work on it in the park one day; he was taking photographs of the New Church or Ayot House through the trees. His camera looked highly complicated to me, and I said as much to him, whereupon he endeavoured to explain the various gadgets to me.

"It looks like hard work, sir," I replied.

"I often forget to move some of them myself," he chuckled, and went on to tell me that these photographs were for the rhyming guide he had mentioned. I felt sorry for him for he looked so old and frail.

"How much do you think we should charge, two and sixpence?" he asked.

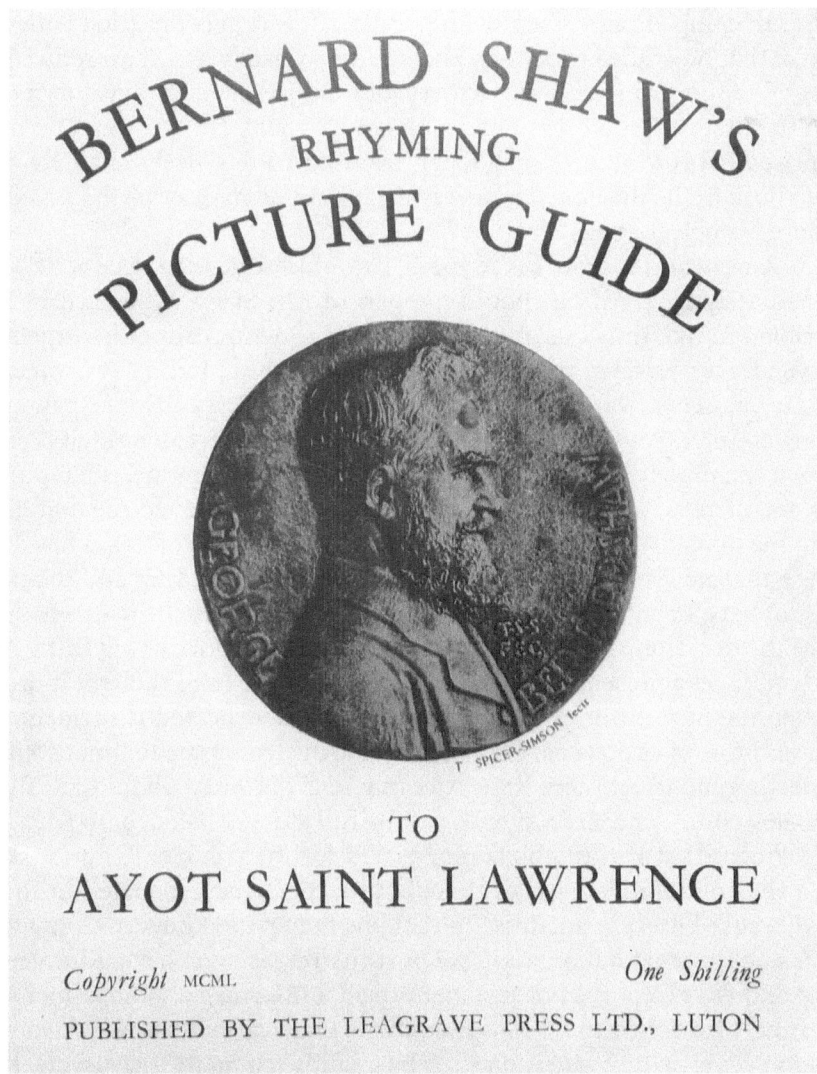

"Oh, no," I replied quickly, "I think a shilling would be quite enough, sir." I thought of the guide as a thin paper pamphlet affair, totally unlike the glossy booklet which it eventually became.

"A shilling it will be then," G.B.S. agreed. And it was. Neither of us knew then that he would be dead before it was published, nor that I would not be the sole benefactor after all, but more of this when the right place is reached.

I had an American nonagenarian in my shop one day; he had flown over from the U.S. especially to call upon G.B.S. with whose vivisection views he was in complete agreement[127] and, indeed, it was in connection with the subject that he wished to see Mr. Shaw. Unfortunately Mr. Shaw refused to meet him, poor old man. I felt so sorry for him. He signed my visitors' book with the first ball point pen I had seen, a very shaky entry it was, and how surprised I was to receive such a pen from him a few weeks later. He had flown back home the next day, a very disappointed man at having failed to achieve his object.

An American reporter asked me if I would promise to telephone him immediately if anything should happen to Mr. Shaw. It seemed rather horrible put like this, but then a man in his nineties cannot be expected to live forever however much regard one has for him. I said "Yes" vaguely, but my vagueness vanished when he put fifty shillings advance payment on my counter. And so, in 1950, when Shaw had his accident I felt bound to earn the money and phoned the number he had given me; the reporter was not there so I asked for the Desk as he had instructed me and gave them the tip, for which they were duly grateful. Apropos of this, a few days before that newspaperman called I had gone to a wedding and, being a hater of hats, I had borrowed a particularly lovely headscarf with which to grace the occasion. The lender informed me, "If you borrow anything like that you'll get a present." That was a new one on me but I thought more of it when the fifty shillings were given to me so unexpectedly. Incidentally, News Editors of various papers also wrote to me from time to time, politely requesting me to let them know the moment Mr. Shaw should fall ill so that they could send a reporter to get the full story. All ended up with the inducement that I would be compensated for my trouble. I cannot say I liked the cold-bloodedness of these approaches. They appeared to think that because I was postmistress I should be the first to know anything that came about—what a reputation we postmistresses must have. I informed none of them except the one just mentioned. I informed another American reporter, who called to my shop seeking a Shaw story, that G.B.S. was in London advertising his new play. "Is he a sandwich man?" he wisecracked. I sent his remark to one national paper as it so tickled me. It tickled them too for it was published.

When Sir Robert Ho Tung[128] came to visit Mr. Shaw, with his wife and secretary, they stopped first at the post office as they were early for their appointment. The secretary, a rather lovely Chinese girl, came in to look at my postcards and it soon came out that she was from Hong Kong. When I told her that I, too, had lived there for some years she was quite delighted and told me who was in the car outside. I was amazed; I had met him casually when I visited his house on The Peak, for their English nanny had been a friend of mine. Incidentally, he was the only

Chinaman allowed to live on The Peak in Hong Kong; others of lower status lived about half way up, while the coolie class were right on the sea level. The girl went out to the car to tell Sir Ho Tung and his wife of this coincidence, and the latter came in to chat for a while before bringing me out to meet her husband. He was now as old a man as G.B.S. although not as agile. He wore his beautiful mandarin clothing, such rich garments although sober in colour, and his mandarin hat brought back many memories to me. The little secretary, however, wore western clothing and very pretty she looked in them.

Another caller to Shaw's Corner was Danny Kaye,[129] whom I would dearly have liked to see although I was in bed ill that day. He did get as far as the village green but the reason I recall his visit was that, for some reason I know nothing of, a press association sent me a guinea, their account note reading "Dany Kaye visits G.B.S." It was a puzzle to me but I pocketed the guinea nevertheless. Wouldn't you? Apparently Danny remained too long talking to Mr. Shaw and was in a mad rush to get back to the Palladium in time for his show there;[130] his car travelled at speed through the narrow lanes only to collide with the innkeeper's one. Danny passed out with the shock but carried on as soon as he recovered. The innkeeper's wife, as she got home, shouted through the window, "The tough guy has fainted!" But I blessed him for my guinea and only wished I had seen him.

I was spending an awful lot of time in and out of bed in those days. I had begun to feel under the weather a long time since for no apparent reason; as time went on I lost weight as well as most of my hair; I became progressively weaker and so shaky that I could hardly raise a cup of tea to my lips without spilling it. A neighbour thought it was high time I did something about my condition and made me call in my doctor, who sent me into hospital next day for observation. I was seen by various specialists, x-rayed from head to foot, and shot backwards and forwards between hospitals until I was giddy, but darned if they really knew what was wrong with me. For a while I was dieted for a duodenal ulcer and, as an out patient, I had to report for regular check ups. The hospital was miles from Ayot and my only means of getting there was either by taxi, which made it expensive, or by the good office of a friendly car owner. Mr. Shaw, however, surprised me by placing his car, complete with chauffeur, at my disposal whenever I had need of it. All I had to do was phone, naming the date and time, and the car arrived outside my gate. The doctors at the hospital were amused to read of this in the newspapers as, of course, it leaked out. "How's your boy friend?" they would ask me playfully. When I thanked G.B.S. for his kindness I told him I was the doctor's dilemma, a point he was quick to appreciate.

Things did not improve. I continued to lose weight, hair, etc. and was again asked to spend a week in hospital for more opinions. I was getting more and more fed up, eventually letting slip that a friend had told me my symptoms were the same as her mother's, who had a goitre.[131] The specialist looked into this theory which, subsequently, proved to be correct; the reason mine proved so hard to detect was that it was an inverted one and not visible in any way. I was prescribed some drug in pill form and sent home, returning every six months to see him. I did not feel very lively during this trying time, but managed to keep the post office going by transferring the business into my living room, where I often had to cope from my bed. I never refused anyone admittance, not even Carleton Smith, the eminent music critic from America,[132] who had been visiting Shaw. He wanted to buy a souvenir of G.B.S. so I entertained him from my sick bed, and sold him an autographed letter from my collection. He struck me as being a particularly nice man and we exchanged letters on one or two occasions afterwards. Indeed I wrote to ask him if he would care to buy a bison's foot but he did not think it a good idea although my letter to him was quoted in full in an American paper. This hoof, by the way, had been a 94th birthday present to G.B.S. but which he passed on to be sold in aid of church funds. His letter accompanying it read: "This knockover jug, a horrible object, was presented to me by Ellen Pollock, who has appeared in my plays with great success. A less suitable present for a teetotaller and vegetarian like myself cannot be imagined. The church here needs heating they tell me. Some person with strange tastes may buy it for enough to fetch a scuttle of coal. So here it is with my blessing. G. Bernard Shaw." The knockover jug, as Mr. Shaw called it, was in fact a bison's foot converted into an inkwell, and was put up for auction at a fête held in the village, but it was not bought by anyone there. The Rector asked me if I could try and sell it in the post office; I sold it eventually to a gentleman from Bermuda, who was a keen Shavian and a writer of plays himself. He came into my office to buy some postcards, and when he saw the hoof and the letter on my counter he was most excited, and made an immediate offer of ten guineas. I had to consult the Rector to see if this was acceptable, which it was, and so these two souvenirs of G.B.S. went off to Bermuda. He must have been pleased with his bargain for I heard from him again several times to know if I had any more interesting Shaw items to sell to him.[133]

In 1948 an endowment policy I held fell due, all fifty pounds of it! Abandoning my necessarily careful ways for once, I decided to blow the lot by taking my first holiday in eighteen years. I invited my sister-in-law to come with me back to my birthplace, Brockenhurst. It was strange to see it again after all those years. The hotel in which we stayed had been the doctor's house and surgery when I was a child; our cottage was still there but six new houses stood in what had been our garden. The village itself was not spoiled for, although larger, it had spread unobtrusively. I enjoyed going over the familiar ground of childhood, but it was a wasted holiday in that I still felt ill. Despite the supply of eggs I had carefully brought with me for eggnogs, etc. Very little stayed down for long.

    I certainly did improve as I continued with my pills, and the specialist eventually told me I need not come to see him again but to carry on with the treatment. By the time Mr. Shaw's 94th birthday came along I was able to participate in it quite actively.

Chapter 9

The newsreel cameramen were in the village on June 28th 1950, intent on obtaining a session with G.B.S. in preparation for his 94th birthday the following month, but they were having little luck in gaining admittance to Shaw's Corner. As usual, they picked on the next best thing, me!

Rather thrilled by the prospect of being a real live film star I agreed to let them run off some of their reel on me. I was arranging flowers in my living room for the scene, the flowers supposedly being my birthday gift for Mr. Shaw. This mild deceit made me chuckle for I did not intend sending any such thing. I well knew Shaw's views on the subject of birthday gifts; "It isn't kind to remind me of my age," was how he put it. The cameramen whiled away their day taking shots of the village and anyone who passed by, hoping all the time for an interview with the leading man. They were still around that evening when I walked down to Shaw's Corner; I particularly wanted to see Mr. Shaw myself on this day, June 28th, and my luck was in for he lingered in his garden just inside the gate. When he saw me he beckoned me to come through, whereupon the newsreel men, hidden from his sight by the hedge, begged me in whispers not to let G.B.S. know they were there. I thought this rather silly of them for if I had asked Mr. Shaw to pose with me at the gate he would have done so. However I did as they asked and said nothing.

"Do you realise, sir," I asked after greeting him, for this was the reason for my call, "I've been getting stamps for you for *twenty* years today?"

Needless to remark G.B.S. was not aware of any such thing, but was suitably impressed now that it was brought to his notice. We chatted awhile of the years gone by and then he asked about my illness. I said that I was much better and, at long last, putting on some weight.

"Never in all my long life have I heard a woman say, with such pride in her voice, that she was putting on weight. How old are you?" he then asked me, curiously.

"Sixty-six, sir," I replied, feeling but a girl again against his great age.

"You're just an infant!" he chuckled, as if he had read my mind.

It was some little time since I had last talked with my old friend for he stayed close to his house now. I was much distressed to notice how his stature had shrunken, and how deaf he had become. I almost shouted to make him hear me. He looked so tired and frail that I felt he would be better indoors and very soon said goodbye and took myself off.

When I came out I found some very delighted newsreel reporters; they had succeeded in "shooting" G.B.S. as he talked to me so I was very much the heroine of the piece. They went home well pleased with their day in Ayot that had not been wasted after all. As for me I was, of course, more than eager to see myself on the screen, not to mention my home and village and last, but by no means least, G.B.S.! However it was no novelty to see him in the news. An evening at the pictures from Ayot St. Lawrence was an outing that took planning at any time and, so that it would not be a wasted journey, I wrote to all the cinemas within a radius of twelve miles asking them to let me know when that particular newsreel was showing. There was some mix up as to whether it would be shown locally at all but, weeks after, it came to Stevenage;[134] off I went with some friends in a state of trepidation. What a very strange feeling it was to see myself moving about in my little cottage and talking to Mr. Shaw in his garden. I felt very proud that I should be included in this birthday excerpt. Those others in the village who had been taken by the cameramen were anxious, too, to see themselves so I was surprised to find they did not appear at all. They must have been cut from the reel presumably. I told them not to bother going as there was only Mr. Shaw and myself to see, and they could see us anytime.

Then, a few days before the much publicised 94th birthday my Head Postmaster phoned me, saying that the B.B.C. had asked his permission before inviting me to take part in a broadcast devoted to G.B.S. After pulling my leg about being a bit of a celebrity myself he said he had given the necessary permission, adding, "You've got a very unusual Christian name."

I laughed and said, "Yes, I think my mother must have thought I'd be a bad lot, meaning Jisbella for Jezebel."

"And are you?" he enquired, amused.

"Certainly not. I'm very good, sir," I chuckled.

This conversation was very soon followed up by a phone call from Valentine Selsey, the producer of the B.B.C.'s "Eye Witness" programme.[135] He wanted to know if it would be convenient for him to come to Ayot St.

Lawrence to record an interview with me at 10.30 next day. Of course whatever suited him suited me, and he was there next morning complete with two radio engineers and their complicated looking apparatus, dead on time.

I felt just a bit weak at the knees knowing I was going to be on the air without any moral support from Mr. Shaw, or anyone else in the village for that matter, but Mr. Selsey's charming manner soon put me at my ease and he had me talking away into the mike with a confident air in no time. He asked the questions and I answered them ad lib, mostly about G.B.S. need I remark, but I also had to tell my own personal story of which you have already read here. When we finished he had the recording played back to me, saying I could make another if I did not like it; it came as an agreeable surprise, therefore, when I heard myself speaking in quite cultured tones with hardly a trace of nervousness. "Well I'm blowed," I exclaimed in amazement, and left the record strictly as it was, and so it went on the air on the 26th July, *the* birthday date in the "Eye Witness" programme; as I listened to myself speaking of Mr. Shaw, I thought how strange that he should be hearing this from London when it was spoken in my cottage such a short way from him, that is *if* he was listening at all. The following Sunday night I unexpectedly heard it all over again on a repeat programme while visiting a friend. Mr. Selsey wrote to congratulate me on the success of my broadcast.

Why pick on me I wondered when, directly after the B.B.C. had interviewed me, the Columbia Broadcasting System of America rolled up with the same request. We all went into another huddle and, beginning to feel pretty experienced at the game, I talked into the mike with even more aplomb than before. The technicians were considerably impressed with the authentic atmosphere of my old cottage and, I could see, were just longing to have some means of making it a vision programme as well as sound. Mr. Paul Niven, who interviewed me, bought one of Shaw's postcards ordering stamps from me for two guineas; when he called to see me again on a later visit he told me he had been offered *five* guineas for it. Well, what's wrong with you, Jisbella, I asked myself. You are slipping a bit, aren't you? From there on I slipped no longer.

I had several letters enclosing stamped and addressed envelopes, asking that I should post them back to the senders on Shaw's birthday and franked with the Ayot St. Lawrence postmark. In all, although I was so involved in Mr. Shaw's birthday celebrations, I never laid an eye upon the man himself on his birthday or, in fact, ever again. Our talk in his garden was to be the last we were to have. On August 29th I received his usual order for stamps but, to my astonishment, he added a final "e" to Lyth, a thing he had never done before. I wondered if his mind were failing at last, but there were no mistakes in his arithmetic when it came to totalling up his order, and his writing was a good deal firmer than for some time past. This was the last stamp order he was to send me.

There were umpteen articles in the press at this time on the subject of Shaw and, in some of them, it was mentioned that I had a large collection of letters from G.B.S. and that I was quite willing to sell them. I expected to have a few enquiries as a result but I did not anticipate reply-paid telegrams staking first claim, nor the scores of letters that followed them. One or two people got hold of the wrong end of the stick and tried to sell *me* Shaw autographs, cards, or letters; others quite blatantly asked me to sell their G.B.S. souvenirs for them on a commission basis. Then, too, there was the writer who suggested he could advertise my wares for me in America at a higher price, and we would split the proceeds although I noticed he wanted 60 percent for his trouble in the matter! Some wanted to buy from me on hire purchase terms[136] while others offered to buy in bulk, or "as many as you care to part with." Some quibbled: were the letters signed G.B.S. or G. Bernard Shaw or George Bernard Shaw; what sort of stationery were the letters written on; what were the contents of the letters and, of course, *how much*? Many came to buy in person. Of course the ones I liked best were those from the genuine Shavian fans, whose letters stood out with their sincerity. I had not realised that I would need my wits about me to this extent, but I tried to sift the wheat from the chaff as best I could. The get rich quick offers I ignored, as I did the hire purchase suggestions and the quibblers. The rest I gave a description of what I had to sell, charging what I deemed their value to the writer. "It is indeed an exorbitant price but I feel it is worth it," wrote one, and that was the general opinion. I sold all but a few, including the last order misspelling my name, which I kept for myself in memory of Shaw. Their sale really put my bank balance in the top drawer, in my own estimation at least.

And so the summer went by and winter began to crawl up my poor old veins again, and then it came, the news that my even more aged friend had fallen, badly. I came to know of it about half past eleven the same morning when his chauffeur came to tell me what had happened, knowing how concerned I would be that our mutually loved benefactor was incarcerated in hospital with a broken thigh.[137] I felt a cold dread. No use to think it is only a broken bone, he will get over it; *he* is not the sort of man it will kill. But he was ninety-four. Why does one expect that he should live forever, just because he is Shaw? Some queer little bug in me seemed to think this was enough. He was eternal. Hadn't he always been there? Wouldn't he always be there? And yet commonsense undermined these thoughts in whispers. Even my dear old friend is mortal, even he must die. How alone I shall feel now without his powerful cloak of protection. But I was being a little premature with my forebodings. Shaw lived. I listened to every news broadcast and hung on every thread of hope passed on from the Shaw household.

My telephone rang incessantly the day G.B.S. fell and, being unable to answer the imperative questions as to how he was, where he was, and why, I took off the receiver in sheer desperation. In the early afternoon I had a visit from a post office official to tell me my phone was now disconnected; he had been unable to cope with the number of calls made to my tiny post office; never before had they been so inundated with calls from the world over, and I mean the world. Everyone it seemed, no matter who they were or what they were, had to know. Who then was he I wondered in awe? Only then did it really strike home how important was the, to me, almost saintly old man who had befriended me since my dear husband died, the sometimes brusque but always thoughtful for my way of life, benefactor. For what else could I call him?

Time dragged by. Quite apart from my anxiety over Mr. Shaw I was feeling ill again myself; mysterious, and very painful, bumps would pop out on any part of my body, and my hands were so tender I could hardly bear to cut a slice of bread. However, I tried to ignore all this and carry on. I had a visit from Mr. and Mrs. Currall, who came with Mr. White, a director of the Leagrave Press, who had been given the task of publishing G.B.S.'s *Rhyming Guide to Ayot St. Lawrence*.[138] I was very much cheered to know that it would be soon ready for sale and, when asked how many books I could cope with, I said that five hundred would be enough to start the ball rolling. Again I envisaged a paper pamphlet and not the glossy booklet with Shaw's head set in a gold medallion on the cover, which it turned out to be.

At last Mr. Shaw was allowed to come home from hospital. Mr. Day dropped by to give me frequent bulleting on how his master fared. The nurses, when they called to the post office, told me that G.B.S. was constantly asking them why they kept him alive, that he wanted to die. Ill myself, this made me even more unhappy. We all knew he could not live much longer.

The world awaited this event, holding its breath, it seemed. Reporters swarmed into the village. About forty of them took up residence in Ayot in order to be on the spot when the moment came. Each house in the village billeted one or two of them; some had beds, some slept on tables, chairs, or on the floors; there were two reporters to each newspaper; while one slept the other waited for news. They were like ants about the village, busily gleaning anything and everything that might appeal to their readers appertaining to G.B.S. while he, poor man, lay near death. It was revolting. They waited three whole days, and the Inn next door attracted many of them; as my living room window is unfortunately near to the men's toilet I heard enough of their callous remarks to have turned my hair grey had it not been so already.

I knew I could not really blame them for their hardness. Their job left them little time for sentimentality. Some of them were nice enough. One ran out of ready cash and came to me for a loan. I trusted him and, sure enough, my money was returned the moment he got back to London.

It was a grey November dawn when I was roused from sleep by thunderous knockings on my door. Opening it I found a bunch of reporters standing there. They told me Shaw was dead.[139] Could they use my phone? I nodded, completely devoid of all feeling now that the blow had fallen. About eight of them squeezed into my tiny room, taking it in turns to phone their editors, each anxious to get in as good a story as the other. And then, suddenly, it was all over. Shaw was dead. There was no longer a reporter in sight. They had vanished. Their job was done. (In all fairness I must add that, before they went, they all walked past Mr. Shaw's body to pay their last respects.) I sat down quietly and tried to realise that G.B.S. was dead. I could not. Next day Valentine Selsey called but as soon as he saw me he realised how ill I was, and he would not bother me to assist in his broadcast.

Mrs. Laden phoned to ask if I would like to come and pay my last respects to Mr. Shaw as the Rector was coming to Shaw's Corner. I felt too ill and grief-stricken and Mrs. Laden understood this. Many of the villagers did go along and give tribute.

The day Mr. Shaw's body was cremated I closed my shop during the cremation service at Golders Green.[140] I put a notice on my door to the effect that this was in honour of G.B.S. A reporter came and copied it into his notebook.[141] Yes, they still looked for morbid details. It was only the second time the shutters had closed over my windows during my stay in Ayot.

About three weeks later Mr. Day came in looking very pale and shaken. I asked him what on earth was the matter. He told me that he, and the gardener, had eaten their midday sandwiches in the garage at Shaw's Corner and, when they finished, went into the garden to carry on with their work. Noticing some ashes scattered in the dell near St. Joan's statue, they wondered what they could be. There was nothing there earlier in the day. Suddenly they knew. They felt shocked that this was all that was left of the man they had known, and loyally served, for so many years. If only they had known beforehand that this was what Mr. Shaw wanted it might not have horrified them so much. As he told me of their discovery my flesh crept although I have nothing against cremation; indeed I intend the same clean ending for myself when the time comes but, somehow, I felt the shock as much as they.

After this I finally admitted to myself that Shaw was dead.

Chapter 10

The village was uneasy now that G.B.S. was dead. There were rumours that Shaw's Corner was to be turned into a shrine for Shavian pilgrims; certainly the house had been given to the National Trust by Mr. Shaw[142] but he left no money for its upkeep, so we wondered and waited. A steady stream of morbid visitors were ever present. Many sought some souvenir to take away with them—stones, earth, hedge clippings, or a piece of grass from his garden. My help was often asked. In their way many of them were sincere enough but it was sometimes difficult to listen to such requests sympathetically. They said that I was fortunate to have mementos of him; indeed my small living room was almost a G.B.S. shrine itself. On every wall hung photographs of Mr. Shaw and Mrs. Shaw that he had given me at one time or another. I mourned for him sincerely and yet I was glad, too, that he no longer had to bear the miseries of his last few weeks.

Life for me went on in much the same way. I still had numerous reporters calling into the post office from far and wide, so many that I could not recall which was which when I received copies of magazines containing the published results of their visit to Ayot; I never knew whether the countless requests for photographs of me were for publication or not. I became accustomed to opening a magazine or newspaper sent me from Holland, Australia, France, or elsewhere, and finding my own picture looking out at me. This, I thought sadly, is Mr. Shaw's last gift to me, fame! I should say reflected glory for, of course, that is all it was.

In early December the B.B.C. Television arrived on my doorstep, expecting to find me all prepared to take part in a proposed programme introducing the *Rhyming Guide to Ayot St. Lawrence*. Apparently I should have been advised of their visit but there must have been a slip up somewhere as it was a complete surprise.

I had no idea that my little pamphlet, as I had come to think of it, would be ready for sale so soon or that it was going to merit all this fuss. It was yet another of those many days that I felt ill and, unprepared as I was, I was not keen on facing up to the television cameras at all. However, rather than upset their programme, I agreed and was interviewed standing outside by the post box. It was a bitterly cold day, and my teeth fairly chattered as I answered the compere's questions as to how G.B.S. had first broached the subject of a rhyming guide and so on. I was in pretty much of a daze and remember little more of the interview. A friend invited me to come along and see myself on TV. I almost wished I had not gone I was so appalled by my own ghastly appearance on the screen. I wrote to the producer to tell him so, as if it was his fault, poor man. He was very kind about it, emphasising that it is often a shock to see oneself on television for the first time!

Mr. Harold White, of the Leagrave Press, opened the programme by introducing "Bernard Shaw's Rhyming Picture Guide to Ayot St. Lawrence," to give it its full title; when he had finished I came into the picture with my part of the story, followed by Mrs. Laden, then the gardener and chauffeur. It appeared that the *Rhyming Guide* was going to be a lot more important than I expected as it was now Mr. Shaw's last completed work, and I realised then that this would mean a fair demand for copies when I got them. I wrote asking for my first consignment to be sent to me as soon as possible. At last they came. I was astonished to find how attractive a little book it was, remarkably good value for a shilling, the price *I* had insisted upon. Looking at it now, I thought that Shaw's suggestion of half a crown would be more like it. It was done now so that was that. How G.B.S. would have chuckled had he seen my face then. I read through it, feeling lonely for the white-bearded figure who had tramped through the village and district with his camera to produce the booklet, the original of which had only been sent to the publishers a few days before he died. I wondered how he could have been bothered to when he was so near to death but I thanked him silently for it; he had not forgotten his promise to give me the *Guide* to sell.

Imagine then my dismay when my paying guest of that time came home to tell me that the *Rhyming Guide* was for sale on every bookstall in Luton. I could not describe my feelings of bewilderment and indignation. I knew that Mr. Shaw intended them to be sold only in my post office. I complained at once to the publishers, and most bitterly, pointing out this fact. Their reply was that, while they realised the book was a result of G.B.S.'s desire to be of help to me, due to his death the demand for his last work would be more than I could manage alone. I cannot say this soothed my wounded feelings much but, as events turned out, I saw the sense of it. From the day the *Rhyming Guides* reached me I was kept busy sending copies of it all over the British Isles. Then *Time* magazine of America took a hand in promoting sales when it included an article on the *Rhyming Guide*,[143] and my name and post office was given full publicity. The results overwhelmed me. Letters asking for *Guides* poured in upon me from every corner of the globe. Envelopes addressed to Postmistress Lyth, Ayot St. Lawrence, England, found me without any trouble—I even got one addressed to the Mayor of Ayot St. Lawrence. I suppose I had as much right as anyone else to be Mayor! In the first mad rush I sent two thousand copies of the *Rhyming Guide* to America alone.

Foreign orders enclosing money in every shape, nationality, and form had me completely foxed; I had to spend an hour with my bank manager to get things straightened out for me. A coin arrived from Tel Aviv but as no one seemed sure of its value, even in the bank, we compromised by selling it to a clerk who was a collector for the price and postage of the *Guide*. With every book I sent a short personal note. It was not necessary I know but, somehow, I wanted all to know a little more of G.B.S. There was a flood of grateful letters, and even gifts, as well as invitations to spend my holidays with the writers; requests for my own autograph came more and more frequently together with the popular demand for the Ayot St. Lawrence postmark. For this I had to get special permission as, of course, franking of letters and postcards is not usually done in a small office like mine. Fortunately, during the peak period, I had my upstairs guests in residence and they helped me out considerably. If ever I needed a couple of secretaries I did then. At times I almost quailed as mail time approached and yet the warmth of admiration expressed for G.B.S. in the letters warmed me too. All envied me because I had known him and they begged me to tell them more of him as a man. Truly now I knew how much G.B.S. had been known and loved. I would like to quote some of these letters. They are stories in themselves, and I cherish them for their sincerity and warmth of heart.

Among the first of the letters from America was this one:

> The December 25th issue of our *Time* magazine, which I receive regularly by mail ahead of issue date contains an article on page twenty titled "Thanks for your Shilling" about Bernard Shaw's *Rhyming Picture Guide to Ayot St. Lawrence,* and illustrated with a half-tone cut of your post office shop from Bernard Shaw's photograph. The article also contains several of Mr. Shaw's Rhyming Verses about his photos of your Hertfordshire hamlet.

I was born in 1886 and will be sixty-five next February 4th. Since I was a boy selling newspapers I have been a devotee of Bernard Shaw and the theatre. One of my earliest recollections is of the great English actor who became an American citizen—Richard Mansfield—in *Arms and the Man*. I have seen every important theatrical production of Shaw's plays in America, and read them all, prefaces included. *Man & Superman, Mrs. Warren's Profession*, Forbes Robertson & Gertrude Elliott in *Caesar & Cleopatra*; also Shaw's wonderful movie productions, with Pascal, *Caesar & Cleopatra, Pygmalion* and *Major Barbara*. In the 1920s I saw the N.Y. Theatre Guild productions of what the *N.Y. Times* now terms *Saint Joan*. I have most of his published works. In 1911 I bought Archibald Henderson's *George Bernard Shaw, His Life and Works*; in 1938 *George Bernard Shaw, Playboy & Prophet*—the second biography by the same author. I have read *The Intelligent Woman's Guide to Socialism* and also *Everybody's Political What's What*.[144]

I heard Mr. Shaw deliver his only talk on his American tour to the American Society of Political Science at the Metropolitan Opera House in New York.[145] As I was also familiar with the life and work of Henry George, including his great book, *Progress and Poverty*, and other works I greatly appreciated the tribute Mr. Shaw paid the inspiration he received from hearing Henry George lecture in London many years ago,[146] and also to his "official" biographer, our own Archibald Henderson. Mr. Shaw's views on Russia at this time have proven painfully prophetic as to what the Communists are doing and threatening to do today.[147]

And—my greatest hobby and vocation has been—photography. So I am interested very much in Bernard Shaw's own *Rhyming Picture Guide* to your home. Today I sent to "Postmistress, Ayot St. Lawrence, twenty-two miles from London, England" a U.S. International Money Order for one dollar, and ask you please send as many copies of this *Picture Guide* as the rate of exchange into your English money—which I do not understand—will allow plus postage by regular mail to my address above. If it does not come out even please do NOT return any money but keep the difference in appreciation of all the good I have garnered from Mr. Shaw's work—for your Ayot St. Lawrence fund.[148]

From the same man upon receipt of the *Guides*:

> Thanks very much for the copies of Bernard Shaw's *Guides*. I am delighted to get these and add to my collection a booklet with photographs made by his own hand, and all the little rhymes about Ayot—which I would like so much to visit one day.

He then went on to give me the story of his own life in more detail, of his family, where he lived, his work, and other interests. We became very good friends by mail. Later he wrote: "Well—now YOU are famous and your picture published in millions of copies of *Life* magazine.[149] I will write and have both *Time* and *Life* mail you complete copies."

These I received in due course although, when returning his cheque to my friend, they pointed out to him that it was against their usual policy to send entire issues abroad; they made an exception in my case as I had been so helpful to them when they were gathering material for their Shaw stories.

Jisbella Lyth in her post office (*Life*, 14 May 1951)

And now for some extracts from an American college girl's letters to me, a correspondence which had quite a delightful and surprising ending:

Dear Mrs. Jisbella Lyth,
I thought you were only a myth.
It now is my pride
To order Shaw's Guide,
A shilling and sixpence herewith.

Her second letter I am quoting in full:

Dear Mrs. Jisbella Lyth
Shaw's book, with your note, did arrive.
Now my Dad wonders if
Your name rhymes, not with myth,
But with something like "Blithe" or "alive"?

Needless to say Shaw's *Rhyming Guide to Ayot St. Lawrence*, not to mention the trouble you went to in sending it, was very much appreciated by the family, all of whom were delighted with the quaintness and humor. There is something very friendly and homey about the little book which serves to keep warm our affection for Mr. Shaw and all that surrounded him. Very lucky you were to have known such an astounding man.

My father, who was very delighted with the *Rhyming Guide*, saw Shaw twice and encountered him once during the '90s. Dad, who had not yet migrated to America, saw Shaw with Chesterton in a debate.[150] The "encounter" took place when Dad, a stranger, accidentally stepped on Shaw's foot in the London Tube. Mr Shaw said "Ouof!!" (He was then red-haired and not yet immortal.) That was as far as the conversation went, I suppose.

I read everything I can of Shaw's and collect everything I can about him. Some day (if I'm ever rich) I would like to visit England and Ayot St. Lawrence, of course, in the bargain.

English stamps are hard to get here. I tried to buy some in a stamp shop and the talky proprietor said "You don't need those, girlie. Get some pretty ones from Argentina." Then I told him about Shaw's *Guide* and your enterprise, but we had a strife finding new English stamps that were still gummy on the backs.

(Poor English people: perhaps they've licked the stickum off because of the food shortage!) Well, we finally found enough for me to send for one *Guide*, but now that I've seen the book I want more for my friends. I'll try sending you a dollar and see if you can send me some, and if there is any change due some gummy stamps.

P.S. All of my professors at the University want *Guides* too, so I told them to get stamps for I don't know how many *Guides* a dollar would buy, if at all."

A third letter:

I wanted to tell you what fun it was to see your picture in *Life* magazine, and I've filed it away in my special box containing items about G.B.S. and friends.

Now I've gradually come into the ownership of five dollars with which I mean to buy some Xmas presents for next winter. You've guessed it. I want some more *Rhyming Guides.* One to a very special friend, who is fond of Shaw. Please send a *Guide* direct to him.

And this was the finale, a letter not from her but from the very special friend:

This belated letter is to thank you for sending me the *Rhyming Guide to Ayot St. Lawrence* which I received many long weeks ago. Since that time I have become engaged to marry the young lady who asked you to send it to me. Perhaps my bride and I will send you a collective letter to thank you for the part you played in bringing us together.

From Yugoslavia:

I read in an American weekly, *Time*, of you and Mr. Shaw's *Rhyming Guide.* If you have a copy to spare could you send it to me? I would be ever thankful to you. I met Mr. Shaw in 1929 when he visited this country,[151] and during three days was at every lunch and dinner with him and Mrs. Shaw. I was his guide. I published my recollections of these days with G.B.S. I have no means to pay you for the desired copy except, at your desire, by international postage.

His next letter:

A couple of days ago I received a copy of Bernard Shaw's *Rhyming Guide* that you were so kind to send me. In it I found your letter telling me what a charming person Mr. Shaw was. You knew him better than I did but, during the three days that I was lucky to be in his and Mrs. Shaw's company, I found them only charming and friendly. I read with keen interest your description of the opening of Shaw's Corner. During the rest of your life you will see many visitors to that corner, where lived and worked one of the greatest men of the twentieth century. And the name of your small but so picturesque Ayot St. Lawrence will live along with Shaw's name. You, personally, can be proud of having enjoyed [the] friendship of such a good and great man.

Thank you many, many times for the precious copy that you sent me. I shall bequeath it to my children as remembrance of a great man their father knew.

P.S. Should any of Shaw's biographers ask you for any material written by Mr. Shaw, kindly let them know that I have in my possession a statement of his, written by his hand and never yet published.

From America:

During my stay in England I visited your village of Ayot and made a call at your post office. I was unable to see you and talk with you as you were down with the flu. I do hope that you have fully recovered now.

The purpose of my visit was to ask if you would be good enough to autograph a copy of Mr. Shaw's last book. I am enclosing a copy of this book and will now ask if you will do me the honour of autographing it on the second page, and accompany the signature with the postage cancellation of Ayot St. Lawrence, and return the book to me.

From British Columbia:

> We were both very sad to hear about Mr. Shaw's passing, and just now we happened to come across an article in *Time* about his last book (*Rhyming Guide to Ayot St. Lawrence*), and rush to place our order for our copy. If the enclosed dollar allows for another copy so much the better. But in any case do not return any change but do with it whatever you see fit. And if you should care to have the mentioned article just let me know and we will send it to you at once. We can hardly wait for the day when we will find Mr. Shaw's *Guide* in our mail.

From Australia:

> I am an admirer of Mr. Shaw and I would much appreciate it if you could let me have a copy of *The Rhyming Guide to Ayot St. Lawrence*. I will enclose a money order for 2/-. If you haven't a copy would you buy a posy with the money and place it at the foot of the statue of St. Joan in his garden, a tribute to Mr. George Bernard Shaw from me.

From America:

> Please find enclosed my check for one dollar for which you may be so kind as to forward me a copy of the first printing of the *Rhyming Guide*. Perhaps, if it is not too inconvenient for you, with your autograph and a late picture of either B.S. or his beloved house. Your autograph will be preserved by me with my Ayot St. Lawrence edition of B.S.'s *Collected Works*.[152]

From America:

> May I ask you to autograph the book for me? I would also like to have an envelope with a postmark of Ayot St. Lawrence. I shall try to send an interesting one for you.

From America:

> Please send me as many of Shaw's *Rhyming Guides* as the enclosed order for ten shillings will buy after the cost of mailing is deducted.

I should be most grateful if you would inscribe one of them with a bit of comment about the Shaw you knew.

From Canada:

I enclose approximately three shillings, and would thank you to forward me at your earliest convenience, two copies of Shaw's *Guide*. I read about this in *Time*.

For your information I would advise that I was born in Welwyn, a few miles from your village, but I have been away for over forty years. I do hope if I ever return for a visit that the old places have not changed too much. As a boy I remember the late Mr. Shaw when he first moved to Ayot St. Lawrence.

From Canada:

Bernard Shaw's *Rhyming Picture Guide* must be a lovely book. I have just read about it in *Time* magazine and I went right to the bank to get a money order.

I am not sure whether I'm glad or sorry to read that Ayot St. Lawrence is "on the way to becoming a shrine." I should love to read that many of the local people have been won over to vegetarianism through their association with the distinguished bard. Ayot St. Lawrence would be a good place for the news to spread throughout the world that all creatures are alike in their right to live and that the world will not stop killing human creatures until they stop killing others.

From Yorkshire, England:

Please send me a copy of the *Rhyming Guide to Ayot St. Lawrence*, and one picture by Karsh, for which I enclose 2/- in stamps.

I have seen your signature but I am interested in your proper name, which I could not decipher from the signature itself. Perhaps you will be good enough to put it in block letters on the leaflet.

From America:

I can't begin to tell you how much we enjoyed receiving three copies of G.B.S.'s last masterpiece! Surely it will go down in history as one of his finest works. But strangely enough, the sequel to this was your darling letter. Somewhere in the letter you wrote, "but I won't bore you with repetition!" Really we did enjoy your letter so much and only hope you will favor us with another. Certainly no one knew G.B.S. any better than you. After all, one can learn more about great people when they are not "on stage" so to speak. It must have been quite an experience to have G.B.S. walk into your post office on a bright sunny morning.

Perhaps, Mrs. Lyth, you are wondering why we feel about G.B.S. as we do. Nothing more than a sincere appreciation of a Great Man with a job well done. Certainly G.B.S. must leave to the youth of today a challenge that will be hard to meet.

I forwarded a little "package" to you this week. Nothing perhaps that you couldn't obtain over there, but we trust that you will enjoy it.

Again let us thank you for sending us the books. And please, when you can find the time away from your various duties, let us hear from you.

From Scotland:

I have been out of town for a week or so and returned to find the box of earth. I was absolutely delighted. Just exactly what I wanted—and from the vegetable garden—lovely! I am grateful indeed.

From America:

The copies of the *Guide* reached me safely yesterday morning, and came as a kind of miracle just as I was completing a paper on G.B.S. to be read that evening before our faculty literacy society. Needless to say, I showed the charming pamphlet and read your intimate and touching notes about the great man's neighborliness, to the great delight of all the members.

I shall treasure the inscribed copy as proof of my belief that behind the rugged mask he presented to the world, there beat a great and kindly heart.

From America:

> Please send me copies of Shaw's *Guide,* as sold in your post office. I prefer the paper-bound copies to the cloth-bound elsewhere obtainable (according to a footnote in *Time*), since to me the actual locale seems to be the more valid and valued source. I am especially keen for the authentic Ayot St. Lawrence booklet for a direct lineal descendant of Catherine Parr (by her re-marriage after the death of Henry VIII).[153] I hope your supply is holding out. If so, and I am not too late to secure three or four copies, will you be so kind as to inscribe your name on the fly leaf on the copy for this friend, and on a second copy for myself?
>
> We are both interested in unusual names—yours is most distinctive. I know you must be inundated with requests but shall be the more appreciative if mine can be granted.

Next letter from the same writer:

> Thank you most appreciatively for your kind letter and most gratifying enclosure of four booklets. I am sorry to hear you have been ill and, while still convalescing, find the avalanche of mail so formidable. I regret having been one of the besiegers under the circumstances. It must be more than any individual can hope to handle and I trust you may have help soon.
>
> The booklets are beautifully produced—from the bronze medallion with the profile on the cover and throughout. I am sending one to the lineal descendant of Catherine Parr, and another to the woman, whose enthusiasm over the first plays of Shaw's produced in this country, led me to an acquaintance with his works. I know they will be delighted to have a copy direct from Ayot St. Lawrence, as am I. It is a beautiful place, where every walk must reward both eye and spirit, so replete with natural charms, old architecture and legends from history and literature. No wonder Mr. Shaw chose it to live in.

From some Americans holidaying in England:

> We appreciated so much your thoughtfulness and courtesy on Thursday, the flowers, the fruits, but above all these and your other gifts, we cherish most your own self and how you made that day seem to be an outstanding one in our lives.

We didn't use all eighteen cards but will you please mail for us those enclosed—airmail—to American friends and with your Ayot St. Lawrence postmark. The enclosed 30/- will cover it all I am sure. If any is left over, go next door[154] and have one or two on us!

From another American caller:

Enjoyed my little chat with you so much. My husband and I will come back toward Spring when your little village should be scenic and sweet. I read my book from cover to cover. It is charming and well worth my forty-mile drive to obtain.

From America:

I'm sending you a newspaper clipping from our paper as I thought you may like to read what an American reporter thinks about your beautiful village.

I was interested to read it but also was distinctly amused for the reporter described me as the postmistress who had presided for no less than fifty-six years! But I will quote no more from the thousands of letters; charming and friendly as so many were, it was impossible for me to continue to correspond with such a vast number.

As my commission on the *Rhyming Guide* is 33 percent, the first sales rush swelled my takings considerably; it has sold steadily but quietly every since. There is also a five-shilling bound copy but I find the shilling one sells more readily nowadays. Later on, when Shaw's Corner was opened to the public, the curator was allowed to sell the bound copies, but I received fourpence on each one sold. The shilling *Guide* remains my prerogative in Ayot St. Lawrence.

Also at this time I was asked to sell busts of Shaw in miniature, a very good likeness, and a companion piece of Mr. Churchill complete with tiny cigar plus spares to give away. So Mr. Shaw and Mr. Churchill sat side by side in my little window, and were a howling success particularly with Americans.

Although quite exhausted by the seemingly never ending demand for the *Guide* I was glad, too, to be kept so busy that I had no time for sad reflections. It was a case of work and sleep in my tiny post office of which G.B.S. in his *Rhyming Guide* had only this to say:

We common people and our betters
Come here alike to post our letters.

Chapter 11

It very soon transpired that I was not going to be the only one so besieged. Much to the dismay of the village as a whole, the National Trust finally decided to open Shaw's Corner to the public. Nobody in Ayot wanted the sightseeing horde which descended upon us during Shaw's last days turned into a permanent fixture; how were we to know that had been a mere drop in the bucket compared to what was to come?

The proposed opening was getting a big build up in the press. Traffic signs went up pointing the way to Shaw's Corner for miles around and we, who had been crying out for some form of transport for years without any success, were to have a bus service at long last. "Takes a dead man to get it for us," I remarked somewhat acidly to one of the many reporters. It looked as if the peace and quiet, which is half of Ayot's charm, was about to be lost to us forever. There was even talk of having one way traffic which would mean a good three mile detour every time we left the village. Before anything happened at all the village folk were up in arms.

A lot of books considered to be of no value were being discarded at Shaw's Corner in the general tidy up, and I went along to look them over. A large photograph album filled with pictures of very dignified Victorian ladies and gentlemen was the first to catch my eye. On the fly leaf Mr. Shaw had written "I do not recognize any of the portraits in this album." His note was dated 1948. Who they were was as much a mystery to me but I decided to salvage it for the sake of the inscription, also choosing another dozen miscellaneous books that appealed to me and which seemed too good to be thrown aside. I felt then that I possessed something that had belonged to G.B.S. which was all I wanted.

A formal invitation to the official opening of Shaw's Corner, arranged for the 17th March, 1951, came in my mail so, on the appropriate day, off

I trotted down the street dressed in my best bib and tucker.[155] In Dame Edith's[156] opening speech she constantly referred to G.B.S. as a rapscallion; she could not have used a better word to describe him and it made everyone there chuckle nostalgically. It seemed so very strange to be standing on his lawn again surrounded by so many people who, had Shaw been alive, would no doubt have caused him to retire to his hut in high dudgeon at such an invasion of his privacy. After the speech-making we were shown through his house, seeing it now as a pubic shrine to a world famous man. Outwardly the rooms looked much as usual but, somehow, nothing about them seemed real any more. Even his weird assortment of hats still hanging in the hall did not move me. Something was missing—G.B.S. It might have been any house of interest.

The opening ceremony was hardly over before the storm broke over us. Cars stretched through the village, bumper touching bumper, the head of an enormous queue filling the narrow lanes for miles; in many places it is impossible for two cars to pass one another without reversing to a wider cut-out but this was out of the question with such an unbroken line of traffic. It was complete chaos although both the police and A.A.[157] men did their best to keep some sort of order. The car park at Shaw's Corner was quite unable to cope with the never ending stream so a nearby meadow was loaned out in an attempt to keep the street clear of cars. Some of them, however, parked wherever they could find space, and as this included the grass lawn outside the Old Ruins Church and beside our small War Memorial, a row of stakes had to be hammered in to protect them. On an average, about a thousand cars a day and their occupants, not counting the regular bus loads also disgorged in the village or the walking parties and cycling clubs, filled Ayot's every nook and cranny. Many of them never got to see Shaw's Corner at all as there was a limit to what the staff there could manage to do.

Villagers found it impossible to get their own cars out on to the road unless they got up very early in the morning and then, by the time they returned after fighting their way through traffic-infested lanes, like as not they were unable to get back in again. Even worse, some of the visitors seemed to think they were on Hampstead Heath[158] on a Bank Holiday, leaving orange peels, empty cigarette packets, and picnic papers all over the place. Surely Mr. Shaw would never have left his house to the nation had he known this was to happen. He loved Ayot St. Lawrence far too well.

Feelings mounted higher and higher.[159] Although I was selling postcards and *Rhyming Guides* as fast as I got them and, such was the demand, even staying open on Sundays to do so, I would willingly have gone without the extra takings to have seen Ayot back to normal. Then "persons unknown" decided to do something definite to show their disapproval and, overnight, all A.A. road signs pointing the way to Shaw's Corner were uprooted bodily and either vanished completely, were broken up, or re-set to point in the opposite direction. This, of course, delighted all the local inhabitants and had the tourists going around in circles. Any of the signs that were hopefully replaced suffered the same fate as soon as darkness fell again. The signs were then withdrawn altogether. Victory to us. If we guessed who had struck this telling blow in our defence we had no intention of giving them away!

An official protest meeting was then called, to be held in the Village Hall, and to which National Trust representatives were invited. It was a stormy meeting of indignant feelings vented in hot words. One solution offered was that Shaw's house should be sold to America. The idea was not taken up. The meeting was widely reported, plus pictures, as far afield as *Life* magazine in America. I had many letters from sympathetic readers who deplored our fate as a second Stratford-on-Avon.[160] However, we were not to be commercialised for even had anyone wished to set up souvenir stalls, or "Pygmalion" tea gardens, Lord Brocket would not have allowed it.

As time went on it turned out that all this panic was quite needless. The worst was over by mid-summer; week by week the thousands gradually dwindled until it was a case of weekends only, and there were no more cars or hiking and biking parties than there had always been. During the week the hust [i.e., quiet] of previous days at last returned. Even our bus, the one good thing resulting from it all, was stopped as it was running at a loss but by then we had become used to shopping sorties made easy for us, and we did not take kindly to doing without it once more. We grumbled, of course, but it did not take long for us to settle back into our long accustomed isolation and [we] managed to get along without it as we had done before.

Listening with half an ear to a favourite radio programme, the Trans Atlantic Quiz between London and New York,[161] and at the same time working out my accounts, I vaguely heard Lionel Hale the question master ask New York, "Who sold £5 worth of stamps at a time to a famous man, and who writes about it?" It took a moment for it to sink in. They could not mean me, I thought in amazement, but listened carefully as it seemed more than a mere coincidence. After several wrong guesses Mason Brown said, "Oh, I know. It was the postmistress of Ayot St. Lawrence, to Bernard Shaw, and Miss Patch writes about it in her book."[162] I nearly dropped my account books with excitement as I heard Lionel Hale ask the name of the postmistress. Would they know? Mason Brown answered, "Jisbella Lyth," pronouncing the name to rhyme with myth. Christopher Morley, who was also taking part in the programme, laughed saying, "With a name like that I should think she came from Havana!"[163] Although all of a tremble I was also a bit disgusted that not one of them had pronounced by name correctly.

Abandoning the accounts, I wrote instead to Mr. Hale, telling him that I liked Lyth to rhyme with blithe, not myth. He sent me a charming letter of apology. My name, he said, was a very unusual one and he imagined I must be a very nice person. Naturally I quite forgave him after reading that.

After all the confusion of the past few months I was more than delighted to find that *Village Wooing* was having a revival at London's Arts Theatre.[164] Brenda Bruce, who was playing in it, wrote, "It adds to the delight of playing *Village Wooing* to know that the lady really exists. I have played a great many G.B.S. parts but this is certainly the most real and human of them." This gave me such pleasure that I felt happier than I had been for many a long day. She invited me to come along to see the show, saying that she would leave the tickets at the box office for me. She sounded a delightful person and I determined to bring her a bouquet of roses from Shaw's own garden. Mrs. Laden, pleased with my idea, sent me down the garden on the morning of the show to pick the roses myself; as I went around the back way I slipped and fell clumsily. "Heavens," I gasped to myself, "I hope this isn't as bad as Mr. Shaw's tumble!" Fortunately, for me it was not, although I did feel pretty shaken, but when Mrs. Laden saw the bruises on my leg she insisted on sending me home by car and promised to pick the roses for me. She sent such a lovely bunch of them.

Determined to do the thing in style I hired a taxi to take the armful of roses, my niece, and me with my bandaged leg, safely to London. As we arrived in the foyer a reporter approached. He seemed to be expecting me. He took us along to Miss Bruce's dressing room where I was able to give her the flowers, which she was enchanted to hear had come from Shaw's Corner. I was completely charmed by her as she chatted, showing me the wigs and costumes she was to wear on the stage that night.

Feeling in need of a drink to sustain me, I went to the lounge with my niece and the reporter, who kept me so busy answering questions on the subject of G.B.S. and *Village Wooing* that it was as much as I could do to get an odd sip of my gin and it.[165] He then asked me if I would pose for a picture with Miss Bruce. Naturally I did not mind a bit but wondered if she would. Reassuring me on this point off we went, and I presented the roses all over again for the occasion. Maurice Denham was also in the dressing room, which was an added thrill for me as I felt that I already knew him from his radio show "Much Binding in the Marsh."[166] When the time came to depart we were escorted to our seats and blinded by more flashes as photographers gave me the VIP treatment. "My goodness," whispered my niece, "everyone is looking at us!" But I was long past being flustered by this sort of thing and settled down cosily to enjoy my evening at the theatre. This time I enjoyed *Village Wooing* tremendously. Seventeen years had passed since it first appeared and, having just met both the actors in it, who had been so sweet to me, I no longer felt at all embarrassed by being portrayed on the stage. If my mind wandered from time to time to the author, who could blame me? The account of my visit, and my picture with Miss Bruce, appeared in the London papers next day.

The third and last time I saw *Village Wooing*, Ellen Pollock played me.[167] This was at a midnight matinee of *Shaw in Heaven* at the Court Theatre, Sloane Square. The seats were e[x]pensive but I was curious to see this new play; I treated myself and a friend to a couple of guinea tickets and, as the hire of a car to London and back cost me another £3, I think this amply demonstrates my high regard for G.B.S.'s memory. I did not, unfortunately, enjoy *Shaw in Heaven* one bit. I thought it in very bad taste but, there, who am I to say so? I brought a nosegay from my garden for Miss Pollock and, once more, watched yet another actress play the part of "Z" in *Village Wooing*. By this time I felt as if I knew most of the dialogue myself. Upon returning, our driver lost his way in the streets of London; we could not find a soul from whom to ask the way at that late hour but eventually found a policeman who set us on the right road. We reached home quite exhausted at four-thirty a.m. Miss Pollock sent me a sweet note thanking me for the flowers a few days later.

But of course I was overdoing things. The mysterious bumps persisted and I continued to lose weight despite the pills I still took religiously; imperceptibly my voice began to change to a husky Tallulah Bankhead[168] tone but, strangely enough, no one in the village noticed this except the baker. In despair I asked for a letter to a London hospital and was examined there by a thyroid specialist. The first question he asked was "Has your voice changed?" As soon as I heard this I had perfect confidence in him. Next he enquired if I had any pills left and, on hearing that I had, he ordered me to toss them in the fire and come back to see him in a month's time. A month went by without the drug. I lost a few more pounds and felt just as poorly as before. At my second visit I was prescribed a new pill; this brought down the swelling in my neck but did nothing to lessen my other complaints. By that time my weight was down to six stone instead of my normal nine stone weight.[169]

Then one night, rather late, I became terribly ill and was frightened enough to phone a neighbour to come to my aid. She took one look at me and called in the doctor. He promptly put me to sleep with an injection and told my friend it was lucky she called me as, otherwise, I might not have lasted the night. I was so glad he did not tell *me*. As it was I was packed into an ambulance and taken to hospital next day. There I stayed for the next two months. Septicemia was the cause of the blobs and bumps apparently, but what they could not discover was what was causing the septicemia. I proved to be a problem case. My niece wrote to say that hearing of my various trips to hospital over the past few years was like the boat race,[170] in—out, in—out!

Treatment banished my bumps and the pains grew less. I was discharged and told to convalesce for a month before having the goitre removed but, before I left, the surgeon came to see me with the news that my London specialist would like to try out a new treatment after my convalescence. I asked his advice. He said that he knew of three cured cases but the treatment was so new that it was still a gamble. To this I replied that I was too old to gamble with my life and would prefer the knife, and I asked him if he would do the job for me. He promised to do so and to make all the arrangements for the operation.

Very much better after my holiday, I wrote to say I was ready for the operation any time he was; in I went on a Wednesday all keyed up to get it over and done with but, by the Friday, the same old trouble flared up again. They removed me very smartly from the surgical to a medical ward and put me on iodine and milk for a fortnight. So puzzling was my case that I had a positive league of nations of doctors continually surrounding my bed. After three weeks of this any hope I ever had of getting better finally left me. I was at the end of the road. I begged the surgeon to operate. He did not think my blood would heal but consulted the pathologist again at my insistence. The pathologist was of the same opinion but I pleaded again for the operation notwithstanding, swearing I did not care which way it went. "We'll let you know in the morning," he replied. That night the Sister told me the night nurse would get me ready. I knew then I was to get my wish and nearly jumped out of bed with joy. Next day I woke up at four o'clock in the afternoon to find my neck encased in plaster. It was all over and I was still alive!

When the plaster was removed in about a week I began to feel more perky. "Now," said the surgeon cheerfully, "we can throw all the drugs on the fire."

My voice was still pretty husky, in fact twice the staff nurse ticked me off for whispering when the doctor came in the ward. "*You* should try having your throat cut!" I croaked indignantly. When it did return to normal I was just a bit sorry to lose my fascinating throatiness.

Whilst still in hospital I had a birthday and, since it fell on a Sunday, some birthday cards arrived for me the day before. I put them on my locker to cheer myself up. Next morning the nurses wished me a happy birthday. I asked Sister if I might be allowed up as a birthday present. "Oh, no, that is impossible," she replied firmly. During visiting hour I saw her busily pushing tables together, making them into one long one. Then out came cups and saucers, about two dozen of them, plus all sorts of fancy cakes, bread, butter, and jam. Chairs were pushed up to the table. I could hardly hold myself from asking what all this was in aid of but did not dare. The moment the visitors left in came Sister bearing a beautiful iced cake, made straight for my bed and dumped the wonder on my knees. "A happy birthday, Mrs. Lyth" said the icing on it. What a wonderful surprise for an old woman feeling just a bit sorry for herself. Matron had a wheeled chair pushed beside my bed, and in it I wheeled to the head of the table where fourteen of us sat down to the best birthday treat of my life. To crown it all I was even allowed to smoke a cigarette at the end of it.

"I can't get out of this bed fast enough," I told the Rector on one of his visits when he gave me the news that the ex-King and Queen of Rumania[171] were coming to live in Ayot St. Lawrence. It renewed my interest in the village and I spent a lot of time wondering if I should ever see them. I need not have worried on that score as I was hardly back in harness before in walked the ex-King himself. He wanted three dog licences and another for his car radio. "Who do I make them out to, sir?" I enquired, pretending not to know who he was although I was pretty sure who he must be.

"One dog for King Michael and two for Queen Anne," was his answer. He did not mention the word "ex." He seemed very shy, and I was thrilled to the marrow to be writing the words King and Queen in my tiny little office, be they "ex" or not.

They were a democratic pair, and were often to be seen walking about the lanes, he in corduroy trousers and sports jacket, and the young Queen in slacks. She brought her three little girls into my office one morning, telling them to sit quietly, while she pored over my stamp folio with great interest. She bought one of each denomination. They were, I suppose, still a novelty to her. The three little princesses might have stepped straight out of a fairy tale so pretty were they, and so beautifully dressed. Our Prince Charles and Princess Anne[172] came to tea with them, although when all the children, and their nannies, walked through the village as far as Shaw's Corner no one took particular notice of the princesses' two playmates. Had we known it was Charles and Anne there would have been much peeping through the windows. Our own Queen came to visit at Ayot House, and when it leaked out that she was coming, many of the villagers watched for her arrival. I, of course, had to stay beside the post office and missed seeing her to my great annoyance.

At a fête held in the village, Queen Anne dressed her children up for the Fancy Dress but would not enter them for a prize. Both the ex-King and Queen partook of village life in the manner born. They were very popular with all of us. When they took up fruit farming we bought our produce from them; Lady Lenanton (Carola Oman, the well known authoress, who lives but a mile or so from Ayot village),[173] ordered some strawberries from them so the King and Queen delivered them, to her back door. Dismayed at this, so the story goes, she told them they ought to have come to the front door. "But we're greengrocers!" was their reply. At another village sale of work I found myself sitting beside the young Queen; we joined forces in trying to guess the name of a doll which was itself the prize for the right answer. Neither of us had any luck.

After all those months in hospital I was very happy to be able to take an active part in life again. I could actually feel myself putting on flesh, a very strange sensation. I let out my two upstairs rooms again as the occasion demanded it as I felt ready to cope with anything. Indeed I felt better than ever before in my whole life.

There were still everyday callers to buy postcards of Shaw and Shaw's Corner, or the *Rhyming Guide*, and they always wanted to chat or to wheedle me into reminiscing about G.B.S. The postcards were rather a sore point just then for the National Trust started to sell them at Shaw's Corner in opposition to me. It got into the press that I had a thousand postcards left on my shelf. That did it. Many people who read this made a special point of buying their postcard souvenirs from me even though they had already visited Shaw's Corner. However, that did not prevent me from becoming friends with the curator and his wife, Mr. and Mrs. Boucher,[174] who had taken over from Mrs. Laden. I found much happiness in giving them a helping hand in the garden that Mr. Shaw had loved so well. I felt I was still serving him in my own small way. After a back-aching weeding session we would walk slowly back to the house for a well-earned cup of tea, Mrs. Boucher reciting "The plowman homeward plods his weary way...."[175]

An American woman lecturer from New York, Dr. Evelyn Newman,[176] called to the post office prior to visiting Shaw's Corner in her search for material on G.B.S. So well did we hit it off that she spent most of the day with me. I gave her lunch and wrote all I knew about *Village Wooing* for her on the back of a photograph showing the stage setting of that play. She was an outstandingly brilliant woman and her lectures, I learned later, were in great demand in the States. She looked awfully like someone I knew but for the life of me I could not think who it was. It was only after I had walked her down to Shaw's Corner that I found out. A villager, seeing her with me, asked if that was Mrs. Roosevelt! Yes, a very brilliant and charming woman, and yet one who enjoyed talking to me in "my adorable cottage so many centuries old."

Another good friend was Rosalind Danecourt, a sculptress encouraged by G.B.S. when she first started working in brass; she made a brass mask and door knocker in his likeness for him, both of which he accepted and that door-knocker is still tapping at the door of Shaw's Corner today.[177] Shortly before he died, she drove up from Cornwall to see him; his last suggestion to her was that she should make a similar knocker for Winston Churchill.

She promised she would and, in time, did so and presented Mr. Churchill with the result. To her joy he accepted it and so her promise to Mr. Shaw was carried out. One of the numerous Treasure Hunting car rallies that are forever picking on poor little Ayot had to find the maker's name on Shaw's doorknocker. As it is printed underneath, there were many inadvertent taps on his door that day. Yet another of these Treasure Hunts had to find out my name. As this is printed over my door it should have been an easy task, but many of them must have been pretty shortsighted or else they could not read. I spent most of the afternoon opening the door to give it in person.

When yet another American caller invited me to go to the States to take part in a film he wanted to make on G.B.S. I was not at all sure how to take it. I could not leave my job, much as I would have liked to investigate such an exciting prospect, and refused. I never did hear any more from him and soon began to wonder if I had dreamed this one up.

One more surprise was when I received a copy of St. John Ervine's book on G.B.S. by post.[178] It was from a lady who said she was a cousin of Mr. Shaw's, but I did not remember ever having met her so that, too, was a complete bolt from the blue.

The following winter I had caught a bad cold but struggled on as those who live alone must do, fetching my firewood and coal from the outhouse. I ended up in hospital again. "Do you know what you've got?" the doctor asked me.

"No," I answered.

"Double pneumonia!" My next of kin were contacted as, for the umpteenth time, I was not expected to last out the night. For the umpteenth time I did. All the nurses and doctors were surprised to have me with them again so soon after my operation.

"The only way we can get rid of you is to shoot you," they chucked.

It made me think of my illnesses in New York so many years ago. They used to ask, "Well, Mrs. Lyth, what are you going to hold your hand out for next?"

During this spell in hospital I discovered that the local newspapers were phoning for news of me. I wondered if this meant I was worthy of an obituary notice and chuckled so much that I began to feel better.

Chapter 12

The jackdaws took advantage of my absence in hospital to build themselves a nest in my chimney, but its foundations seemed to be very insecure as sticks, stones, bits of glass, and old bones came showering down into my fire for weeks. Eventually, in the middle of a bitterly cold winter's night, the whole lot caught fire. I jumped out of bed and flew to the phone for the Fire Brigade. They came within fifteen minutes, by which time I was dressed and fluttering about in a great panic. The roar of the fire in the chimney terrified me when I thought of the old beams just waiting to burst into flame; the firemen put it out in no time but made a terrible mess. I did not mind the mess a bit when they confirmed what I had been thinking—the cottage would have burned to the ground had I not woken in time. The rest of that night I spent in the Inn next door, the firemen finishing off my rescue by carrying my divan bed over there for me. The curator at Shaw's Corner loved to tease me by telling the story, ending up, "Not only do the jackdaws collect sticks for Mrs. Lyth but they even light the fire for her."

Never a dull moment, I thought, when I heard the B.B.C. wanted me to broadcast again, this time on their Italian network. The subject? Well, can you guess? I was not quite sure why they picked on me for this one but I obliged, and was paid two guineas for it. This was indeed a surprise as I had never been paid for any other recordings but, nevertheless, I pocketed it thankfully. Whether this was responsible for starting me thinking of foreign travel again I am not quite sure, but start thinking I did. I was feeling well for the first time in five years. My finances were in pretty good repair as a result of my wonderful collection of G.B.S. letters principally, and I thought it was time I enjoyed myself. I wondered if the Continent was all it was cracked up to be and, there being only one way to find out, I booked a holiday in Switzerland by *plane*. I had never flown and I was seventy-one.

High time I did. I wrote to a friend telling her of my plans, saying that I had gone completely mad. She replied, "My dear, that is the only way to keep sane." We were in complete agreement.

All of my friends and relations were dead against me taking to the air at my advanced old age, but it was one more thing I meant to do before I died. Just before my departure, I sent them postcards saying that I would already have reached Switzerland, if the plane did not crash, by the time they read them. What a wonderful experience that first flight was. The ease and luxury of it thrilled me as much as the actual take off when I gasped to see the airport disappear beneath us, and how I revelled at being in the heaven of bright blue sky and snow white clouds gilded gold at the edges by the sun. I longed to get out and walk on those cotton woolly formations that looked so solid. I loved every minute of the trip, catching my breath in awe at the picture postcard beauty of Switzerland as we came in to land at Basel. My admiration for the pilot's skill was complete when I found we had touched down while I was still waiting for the bump to announce the fact.

A luxury motor coach was waiting at the airport to take me and my fellow tourists on to Interlaken, where we spent a glorious five days. I had joined an organised tour, knowing that I should be well cared for and would not lack companionship but, of course, I was the oldest of the party. They were a grand lot of people who took me to their hearts right away when they saw I meant to keep up with them come what may, and did not jib at anything. I went up mountains by chair lifts and gazed in awe at glaciers and snow covered peaks whilst I shivered in my thin coat; I basked in the sunshine as we boated on lakes and watched the thousands of trout mill around us; I walked through the lovely alpine meadows where the crickets chirped merrily; on hazardous mountain coach rides I closed my eyes at the yawning chasms alongside, opening them from time to time to drink in the marvels of nature around me. In Interlaken I was introduced to the mysteries of roulette but my luck was not in unfortunately.

The rest of the trip was divided up between Lucerne, Bern, and Zurich. Our Lucerne hotel had once been visited by Queen Victoria and, indeed, the interior had a very English flavour and was dotted about with knights in armour. For the rest of the tour I was nicknamed Queen Victoria but I *was* amused.[179] How everyone pulled my leg but what very good care they took of the adventurous old lady just the same. I quite fell in love with Switzerland, and would willingly have lived there forever but little Ayot claimed me back within the stated time of post office holidays. I swore that I would return again next year.

When King Michael and Queen Anne left for Switzerland later on in the year I was so very envious, sighing to think of the lovely winter months they would spend there. It was only a while later that we heard King Michael had decided to live there having taken a post with a Swiss aircraft firm. Queen Anne came back alone in the New Year to organise the removal of their furniture from Ayot House and very soon the big house stood empty once more.

In the quiet winter months nothing much happens in Ayot apart from frozen water supplies and falls of snow, so someone new to talk to breaks the monotony. When, just after Christmas, a youngish couple with a little boy moved into the cottage beside the Old Ruins Church I was glad to chat with the young woman who came to buy stamps and beg shillings for her electric meter.[180] As time went on we became friendly. Irish herself, she was interested in G.B.S. knowing Torca Cottage well,[181] it being a stone's throw from her home in Ireland. She was always interested to hear me reminisce about him and about my own travels, at least she was polite enough to give me that impression. Telling me she was going to a local dogs' home to look for a Labrador dog, I was surprised to see her appear with a lovely Collie. She had quite fallen in love with its sad eyes and wagging tail. A little later an account of this love story appeared in a country magazine which was how I found out that Romie, as she made me call her, liked to do a bit of writing when she had time. Her young son[182] saw to it that she had little to spare.

Meanwhile Shaw's Corner was leading a pretty quiet life after its hectic opening five years back; there were frequent small paragraphs in the press that the house was to let to a suitable tenant, a condition being that they must open to the public on certain days. The rent was low but the rates were high.[183] Every so often the village grapevine announced that this person or that had taken it, or that it was to be turned into a Shavian club, or that a fabulously rich American intended to run the house as a home for aspiring dramatists. There were rumours, too, about Ayot House but one guess was as good as another, and nothing concrete happened to either house for some time. It was something of a surprise then when my friends the Bouchers announced that they were leaving Shaw's Corner, that the house had been let. Nearly all of Shaw's furnishings went with them to another National Trust property, leaving only the hall, study and hut as G.B.S. had left them. The new tenants, Mr. and Mrs. Casserley,[184] were a young couple with two small boys.

As this summer of 1956 was Mr. Shaw's centenary year, Mr. Boucher had been kept pretty busy before he left. There was a revived interest in G.B.S., Shaw's Corner was televised for the occasion, and there were quite a few Shavian pilgrims to the village but not as many as we expected. Reporters asked me if Ayot St. Lawrence was not staging some celebrations for Shaw's centenary. I had to chuckle. Little did they know Ayot. It does not go in for such things. In any case I was having a private celebration by taking myself away from Ayot, sallying off to the continent for another glorious fourteen days of adventure.

This time I had booked a more ambitious tour, starting with a flight to Basel and then a marathon mileage by coach through Switzerland, Austria, Germany, Lichtenstein, and into Italy; we had one night stops from Basel to Vienna where I actually slept two nights in the same bed. Our passports never seemed to be out of our hands. When we got to Venice my ankles were swollen but I was determined to miss nothing. We went by gondola in and out of hundreds of water streets; we took a motor boat up the Grand Canal to see how Venetian glass was made; we saw where Marco Polo lived, we passed under the Bridge of Sighs, passed the Salute Church where the young Princess Ira was married, and then I crawled into bed. Next morning we hired a guide to show us anything we had missed the day before, starting off with the Doge's Palace. The guide, pointing out a secret door leading to the Bridge of Sighs, said darkly, "When they went through there they never came back!" That was where I passed out.[185]

My next view of Venice was an odd one. I was sitting on a chair which was being carried to an ambulance boat by some Red Cross men. Three of my tour companions came with me to the hospital where I was set down in a public ward. None of us spoke Italian and none of the hospital staff spoke any English. My friends gesticulated frantically for an interpreter and, after much ado, our courier was contacted. By the time she came I had already been given an injection, and only wanted to get back to my hotel bed. I was allowed to go on condition that I saw another doctor at the hotel. This one not only spoke English but told me firmly I could not continue the tour, and that I must go to the hospital next day for rest and treatment. I was suffering from complete exhaustion.

To hospital I went next day feeling very alone and somewhat frightened but, once I felt a little better, I quite enjoyed the experience. The Sister, or Signorina as they called her, and I managed a sprightly conversation with the aid of a phrase book which she proudly presented to me. I was looked after beautifully and the British Vice-Consul, a lady, who had been informed of my presence in Venice, came to supply me with books and, most precious gift, a packet of tea. The Sister brought me a little teapot, so with my national beverage to comfort me the next two weeks went by quite happily. The Vice-Consul booked a hotel room for me where I went to recuperate when I was discharged as fit, and there I rested a few more days. When the Vice-Consul told me that she had a friend staying with her who knew Mr. Casserley, the new tenant of Shaw's Corner, and sent a message to him with me I thought, "Even here I can't get away from my connections with Shaw." I flew home very successfully although I did need a few whiffs of oxygen over the Alps, but I was as right as rain when we got back to 8,500 feet.

Ayot seemed a little surprised to see me back again looking reasonably hale and hearty. Many of the villagers had given me up for dead long since, but they ought to have known they could not get rid of me so easily. In next to no time the long promised repairs to my roof were started. Every bit of it was removed, and the dirt and dust of ages cascaded down the stairs and had me coughing and choking like a person with asthma. With only a sheet of roofing felt between me and the skies above the cold was intense. I shut myself into my downstairs living room and tried to ignore the next two weeks. The only good thing about the whole episode was that it did not rain. However, once it was done I was more than pleased and felt a deal more secure.

Next item on the agenda was the news that Ayot was to have a Silk Farm! Zoe, Lady Hart Dyke,[186] whose Lullingstone Castle Silk Farm was famous as the only one in Britain and for having supplied the silk for our Queen's Coronation Velvet, was moving into Ayot House complete with millions of embryo silk worms. Everyone started swotting up on the subject, discovering that approximately eighty thousand visitors came to see her farm each year. The village was aghast. First Shaw's Corner now this, was the general feeling.

Lady Hart Dyke arrived shortly before Christmas, and was soon to be seen striding energetically about the village, followed by a large Airedale dog, or dashing smartly down the lanes on her little motor scooter. We were quickly charmed by her amusing personality and vitality but, notwithstanding, a meeting was called to deal with the threat of yet another tourist invasion. Lady Zoe explained that she, too, had fallen in love with Ayot St. Lawrence and had no wish to see it spoiled; she assured us that she would do everything she could to keep cars and buses visiting the Farm within her own grounds, and would make a car park big enough to hold them. The Silk Farm's "open" season was in the summer months only we learned as, in this awful climate of ours, silk production relied on warmer weather. If the mulberry leaves, upon which the baby worms are reared, are not ready at the right time or get spoiled by frost, then the poor little things must die.

Picture our amusement when it materialized that Shaw's Corner was joining forces with Lady Zoe; her opening day on the 1st of April [1957] was to be in conjunction with the re-opening of Shaw's Corner. For this, the drawing and dining room furniture was brought back and put into their original places as in Shaw's day. So it was arranged and so it took place.

News of the double event was televised and in the press. Lady Hart Dyke spoke on the radio in "In Town Tonight"[187] and made us laugh as she described the antics of the enormous Russian moths which had just hatched out from some eggs lately arrived from Russia. The only trouble was that no instructions for feeding had been sent with them. She tried them with everything but, in the end, the lovely things with a wing span of six or seven inches all died. They had flown madly about and stuck themselves to the high ceilings and picture rails, from which Lady Zoe and her staff climbed perilously to catch them.

Actress Jill Adams, accompanied by her fiancé Peter Haigh,[188] performed the opening ceremony of the Silk Farm, and then Lady Hart Dyke swept us enthusiastically into the first tour of the Farm. After this, everyone trooped through the village to Shaw's Corner, where Miss Blanche Patch ceremonially re-opened it. Esmé Percy,[189] the well known-actor who played so many G.B.S. parts and who was President of the Shaw Society, was there. I was so pleased to meet him again and to chat awhile of Mr. Shaw. What a shock I got a scant six weeks later to hear that Mr. Percy had died suddenly. Another link was broken.

The threatened invasion was not unbearable after all. There were quite a few coaches but they hid discreetly inside the gates of Ayot Park, and there was no all-out influx by car such as we had suffered before. Lady Zoe also opened a tea room and a snack bar at Ayot House and, indeed, on a fine Sunday afternoon I enjoy taking tea there and looking out over the lovely garden, something it never occurred to me I should be privileged to do twenty-seven years ago.

There is little left for me to say. Essentially, Ayot alters not at all. The Shavian fans still call upon me, and reporters still hope to dig up something new on G.B.S. What I have to say they can now read for themselves, and pester me no more with their questions. I look forward to a peaceful old age, and have it all nicely planned to retire when the time comes to one of those charming alms houses, where I need be a burden to no one but myself!

NOTES

1   Shortly after Shaw's death, a Shaw enthusiast named Allan Chappelow (1909–2006) began interviewing people who had known Shaw in Ayot St Lawrence and the surrounding area. Among them was Jisbella Lyth. In the interview she speaks very briefly about her life before moving to Ayot in 1931. Publication of Chappelow's collection of interviews—*Shaw the Villager and Human Being. A Biographical Symposium* (London: Charles Skilton)—was delayed until 1961. Jisbella's interview is on pp 80–91. Chappelow also published a companion volume to *Shaw the Villager* called *Shaw "The Chucker-Out": A Biographical Exposition and Critique* (London: George Allen & Unwin, 1969). Jisbella Lyth is a character in *Proud* (2013), a political satire by Canadian playwright Michael Healey, though Healey's rumbustious and raunchy character is about as far removed from Postmistress Jisbella as it is possible to imagine.
2   The nearest towns are Southampton (20 km to the north-east) and Bournemouth (25 km to the south-west).
3   A rubber-like latex.
4   A popular late nineteenth-century American poem (author unknown) published variously as "Write Them a Letter Tonight" and "The Old Folks' Longing."
5   An annual dog show (established in 1891) held at the Earl's Court Exhibition Centre in London.
6   A low bed on wheels that can be stored under another bed.
7   A style of moustache extending across the upper lip, and then down each side of the mouth in the shape of a figure eleven.
8   A leading London-based opera company formed in 1873 by German-born Carl Rosa (1842–89). In addition to "Carl Rosa. The Artistic Merits and Shortcomings of the organiser of English Opera" in *The Star* (1 May 1889), Shaw wrote nine reviews of Rosa performances (seven in 1890).

9   The second Boer War (1899–1902) fought between the British and the Boers (South Africans of Dutch origin) for control of South Africa, ending in British victory with the capture of Pretoria in May 1902.
10 Presumably Jisbella's other admirer.
11 A village about 80 km north-east of Southampton.
12 The honeymoon appeal of Princes Risborough must have been strong to justify a 50-mile (80-km) bicycle ride (directly north of Ash).
13 Built in 1895, the *Borneo* was part of the fleet of the Peninsular and Orient shipping company, founded in 1837. Jisbella provides but a scant description of her voyage to Hong Kong, but it takes her south across the notoriously stormy Bay of Biscay, through the Strait of Gibraltar into the Mediterranean, then through the Suez Canal (opened in 1869) into the Red Sea, across the Indian Ocean to Sri Lanka (which she would have known as Ceylon), then to Penang and Kuala Lumpur (Malaysia), Singapore, and, finally, north through the South China Sea to Yokohama before doubling back to Hong Kong. (Jisbella gives an itinerary that places the stop at Singapore ahead of those in Kuala Lumpur and Penang, but that seems unlikely.)
14 It is strange that Jisbella says nothing about her first stay in Hong Kong, which lasted nearly three years. At some point during that stay she was employed by William Bradley Walker (an executive with Standard Oil in Hong Kong) and his wife to help care for their three young sons.
15 Jisbella's voyage from Hong Kong to Vancouver was on the Canadian Pacific ship *The Empress of Asia*, which stayed in passenger service until converted to a troop ship for World War II. She was sunk by Japanese aircraft on 5 February 1942 en route to Singapore. Jisbella's itinerary to Vancouver included the Sea of Japan (the west coast of Japan), Yokohama (east coast of Japan), and Manila (Philippines, south of Japan), though in what sequence she doesn't make clear.
16 A polio epidemic broke out in New York (and other parts of America) in the summer of 1916. There were over two thousand deaths in New York.
17 When it opened in 1908 the New Washington quickly established itself as the premier hotel in Seattle, favoured by American presidents (and Elvis Presley) on their visits to the city. In 1963 the hotel was converted to low-income housing.
18 A chain of department stores, launched in Seattle in 1890.
19 The Orpheum Theatre opened as the Alhambra Theatre in 1909 at 5th Avenue and Pine Street. It became part of the Orpheum Theatre circuit in 1916, and was renamed the Wilkes Theatre in 1917.
20 The Evangelical Church is now (2018) known as the Gethsemane Lutheran Church.
21 The Iroquois Hotel is still (2018) in business at the same address.

22 The Metropolitan Opera House was located at 39th Street and Broadway when Jisbella heard Italian tenor Enrico Caruso (1873–1921) and Italian soprano Luisa Tetrazzini (1871–1940) sing there.
23 Jisbella saw Russian ballerina Anna Pavlova (1881–1931) dance at the New York Hippodrome (opened 1905) on 6th Avenue between West 43rd and West 44th Streets.
24 Annette Kellermann (1886–1975) was a multi-talented Australian swimmer, actress, and vaudeville star. Jisbella saw her in the silent movie *The Daughter of the Gods* (1916) at the Lyceum Theatre on West 45th Street between 6th and 7th Avenues.
25 Neither Mary Pickford (1892–1979) nor Douglas Fairbanks (1883–1939) appeared in the silent movie *20,000 Leagues Under the Sea* (1916), but Jisbella would have had plenty of opportunities to see the two early Hollywood stars in other movies.
26 Kingsley School for Boys, Essex Fells, New Jersey.
27 The United States declared war on Germany on 2 April 1917 after Germany targeted all ships trading with Great Britain, including American ships.
28 Emery Rice was captain of the merchant ship SS *Mongolia*, which sank a German submarine in the English Channel on 19 April 1917. The New York celebrations took place on 16 May 1917 (as reported in the *New York Tribune*, 17 May 1917).
29 An infection of the mouth, throat, and gums (named after French physician Henri Vincent, 1862–1950).
30 A communicable disease hospital on East 16th Street along the East River. It was named after the American surgeon Willard Parker (1800–84), and was in operation from 1885 to 1958.
31 Founded, by bequest, in 1871 by James Henry Roosevelt (1800–63) on 9th Avenue and West 59th Street. It is now (2018) operating as Mt Sinai West Hospital in a different building but adjacent to the original site.
32 White Plains and Pelham are in Westchester County, just north of New York City.
33 A beach area in Brooklyn, enjoyed by Jisbella a few years before the famous Coney Island entertainment park opened in 1923.
34 West Point, on the Hudson River, is more formally known as the United States Military Academy, founded in 1802 by President Thomas Jefferson. George Washington's plantation home, Mount Vernon, is on the Potomac River.
35 St George's Anglican Church in downtown Montreal was founded in 1843. "Abide with Me" is a mournful but popular hymn written in 1861 by Henry Francis Lyte.
36 Moose Jaw is a small city in southern Saskatchewan.
37 Probably Hell's Gate in the Fraser Canyon.

38	Founded in 1913, the Vancouver Club is an exclusive private club in downtown Vancouver.
39	The *Monteagle* was built in 1899 and remained in service until 1926, primarily on Canadian Pacific's trans-Pacific route.
40	The *Monteagle* crossed the international date line (180th meridian) going east and so lost a day.
41	"Jesus Shall Reign" is another popular hymn (more lively and uplifting than "Abide with Me" [note 35]), written in 1719 by Isaac Watts.
42	Where Japanese women (geisha) provide traditional entertainment and refreshments.
43	Founded in 1869 and still (2018) a leading school in Kowloon, a suburb of Hong Kong.
44	The tragedy described by Jisbella occurred on 26 February 1918. "The records of Hongkong contain no parallel to yesterday's disaster," the *South China Morning Post* reported (27 February 1918), while the headline on the same date in the *Hong Kong Daily Press* was "TERRIBLE CATASTROPHE AT THE RACES."
45	Midday meal (Indian English).
46	An infectious skin disease.
47	The earthquake occurred on 13 February 1918. It wasn't as bad as Jisbella thought. There were no deaths and only minor damage to buildings.
48	The highest point in Hong Kong (554 metres).
49	Astor House in Gwulo, Hong Kong. The New Astor Hotel opened in 1958.
50	Fan-Tan is a traditional Chinese gambling game that is far too complex to describe in an endnote, though Jisbella seems to have mastered it well enough to win some money. (There is a helpful Wikipedia entry.) Macau Island, an hour's ferry ride west of Hong Kong, has come to be known as the Monte Carlo of the East.
51	Built in 1914 for the French company La Compagnie des Messageries Maritimes, the *Sphinx* served as a hospital ship in both world wars. Jisbella's voyage took her from Hong Kong to Haiphong and Saigon (now Ho Chi Minh City) in Vietnam, to Colombo, and then west into the Gulf of Aden and the Red Sea and through the Suez Canal into the Mediterranean Sea. After the dangerous passage through the Strait of Messina (avoiding unexploded First World War mines, and passing by—to Jisbella's disappointment—a dormant Mount Etna), the *Sphinx* docked in Marseilles (its home port).
52	Le Havre is 200 km northwest of Paris at the mouth of the River Seine. The 230 km crossing to Southampton would have taken at least fifteen hours.
53	About 5 km southwest of Ayot St Lawrence.
54	The "old man" was sixty-two.
55	A coastal resort town in Sussex, about 90 km south of London.
56	Am's sister lived in Whitby, on the north-east coast.

57   A Yorkshire town about 100 km south-west of Whitby.
58   Yorkshire's largest city.
59   Payment by instalments. See also note 136.
60   A town near Leeds, about 100 km south of Harrogate. Jisbella and Am would have travelled by train.
61   Conservative Clubs are private clubs for members of the UK Conservative Party. Bradford is about 30 km south of Harrogate.
62   Slate clubs were groups of friends—without the means to hold a bank account—contributing to a common fund (held by a trusted member of the group) to save money ("putting it on the slate") for re-distribution at a later date when the money was needed (e.g., for summer holidays or Christmas). (Putting something on the slate—or "tab"—can also work as a temporary debit system.)
63   Charles Nall-Cain (1866–1934), a wealthy businessman and philanthropist, was made Baron Brocket of Brocket Hall (in Ayot St Lawrence) in 1933. Much of his wealth came from the family brewing company, hence the re-naming of the Brocket Arms in 1934 (see note 69).
64   According to Ayot St Lawrence historian A.W. Tuke (see Chappelow 338–44), the story of Sir Lionel Lyde's (1724–91) wanton destruction of the twelfth-century church in Ayot (and the Bishop's intervention) is based on "local tradition" only—though Lyde and his wife are indeed buried as Jisbella describes. Nicholas Revett (1721–1804) designed the New Church (1788) in the Greek Revival style of London's St Pancras Church, but the St Pancras church was designed by William and Henry Inwood, and in any case construction did not begin until 1819, well after Revett's death. (See *Welcome to St Pancras Parish Church* [n.d.], published by the church.) Jisbella's statement is, however, supported by Tuke (Chappelow 342).
65   A sister village to Ayot St Lawrence, a few minutes to the south-east.
66   The bar. The pub would have been closed on Sundays.
67   According to A.W. Tuke, local tradition has it that Henry VIII once imprisoned his second wife, Anne Boleyn, in the manor house (before beheading her in 1536). This "charming story," as Tuke calls it, is in Chappelow 343. There is no record of the current whereabouts of either Henry's hat or Anne's shoes. Shaw's *Rhyming Guide* (12) relates: "Here they two danced and kept their carriages / And hunted long before their marriages, / Not dreaming that Ann's elevation / Would end in her decapitation."
68   Captain L.G. Ames lost his left arm in action in the First World War. His family owned the rectory that Shaw initially leased (1906) and then purchased (1920) as his country home. Ames records his occasionally testy Ayot relationship with Shaw in Chappelow 144–59.
69   The name of the village pub was changed from the Three Horseshoes to the Brocket Arms in 1934, when the Harding family bought the property. Mrs

Harding's recollections of Shaw are in Chappelow 92–97: "Mr Shaw often met his friends here in the Brocket Arms"—though as a lifelong teetotaller Shaw never drank alcohol (in the pub or anywhere else). Shaw refers to the change of name in his *Rhyming Guide* (7): "Your tea [sic!] take at the Brocket Arms. / As The Three Horseshoes it was famed / But after two World Wars' alarums / It was baronically renamed."

70   Jisbella was buried in the same grave when she died in 1964.
71   A neighbouring village, with the closest Catholic church to Ayot.
72   Actress Connie Ediss (1871–1934).
73   Several photographs of Shaw swimming and sunbathing in Antibes on the Côte d'Azur in the summer of 1928 were either taken for or sold to the Keystone Press Agency. Some are reproduced in Chappelow 282.
74   According to Blanche Patch, Shaw's secretary from 1920 until Shaw's death, "it was the villagers who first called the house Shaw's Corner" (Patch 34).
75   Fred Day was Shaw's chauffeur from 1931 until Shaw's death. His recollections of Shaw are in Chappelow 37–47.
76   In addition to his home in Ayot St Lawrence, Shaw kept a flat in London (4 Whitehall Court) from 1927 until his death.
77   Two-and-a-half pence.
78   There is ample evidence of Shaw's generosity in Ayot St Lawrence in the recollections of his neighbours. Novelist and biographer Carola Oman (1897–1978), for example, commented that "Shaw was a generous man and he was regarded as such in the village. He gave to all the village funds" (Chappelow 160).
79   The tombstone of Mary Ann South in Ayot indicates that she died on 5 March 1895 at age seventy, and adds that "Her Time was Short." Shaw outlived her by twenty-four years.
80   Thomas Edward Lawrence (1888–1935), who became a close friend of Shaw. The relationship is the subject of Stanley Weintraub's *Private Shaw and Public Shaw* (New York: Braziller, 1963).
81   I.e., there was no choice. Given the rationing of meat, it was vegetables or nothing for the unfortunate dogs.
82   Ivo L. Currall (1902–60) was a lawyer who helped Shaw with copyright and other matters, and was an avid Shaviana collector.
83   Fritz Erwin Loewenstein (1901–69) was a German refugee who established himself at Shaw's Corner as Shaw's bibliographer—with resistance from Blanche Patch—and founded the Shaw Society in London in 1941, which is still active (shawsociety.org.uk).
84   One of Ted Orme's photographs is on the front cover of this book.
85   Jisbella compares herself unfavourably to the British actress Gladys Cooper (1888–1971).
86   Britain's National Health Service was established in 1948.

87 Shaw wrote *Village Wooing* in early 1933. It was first produced in Dallas, Texas, on 16 April 1934. The first British production was in Tunbridge Wells, Kent, on 1 May 1934. It was first published in a German translation (*Ländliche Werbung*) in 1933, and in English in 1934 as part of the *Collected Edition* of Shaw's works (volume 31, with *Too True to be Good* and *On the Rocks*). *Village Wooing* consists of three "conversations": the first takes place on a "pleasure ship," and the second and third in "a Village Shop and Post Office on the Wiltshire Downs." There are only three characters: a deck steward (unnamed), "A" (male), and "Z" (female).

88 The production of *Village Wooing* that Jisbella saw was the first London production of the play. It opened at the Little Theatre on John Street (now John Adam Street), just off the Strand, on 19 June 1934. The deck steward was played by Edward Wheatleigh, and the two principal characters by Arthur Wonter (1875–1960) and Sybil Thorndike (1882–1976). The Little Theatre was destroyed by enemy bombing during the London blitz in 1941.

89 John Galsworthy's (1867–1933) *Little Man* was first produced at the Birmingham Repertory Theatre on 15 March 1915.

90 Blanche Patch's account of the composition of *Village Wooing* is on pp 74–75 of *Thirty Years with G.B.S.*

91 The Jisbella Lyth collection includes a typed transcript of the article, in which Jisbella is described as "a business woman with an arresting manner."

92 The Malvern Festival (in Worcestershire) was founded by Sir Barry Jackson (1879–1961) in 1929 as a showcase for Shaw's plays, many of which premièred there. Shaw became a close friend of Jackson and was a frequent visitor to Malvern. See *Selected Correspondence of Bernard Shaw: Bernard Shaw and Barry Jackson*, ed. L.W. Conolly (Toronto: University of Toronto Press, 2002).

93 The *Tatler* is a fashionable society "lifestyle" magazine founded in 1901. The article referred to by Jisbella, with several photographs, appeared on 16 November 1938, pp. 28–29.

94 Jisbella does not name the newspaper, but there were several with *Daily* in their name: *Daily Telegraph*, *Daily Mail*, *Daily Express*, *Daily Mirror*, and *Daily Herald* among them. Given Jisbella's fondness for the crossword in the *Daily Telegraph* (*Postmistress*, p. 76), it is likely that this is the paper she had in mind.

95 Great Britain declared war on Germany on 3 September 1939.

96 A popular British way of referring to German flying bombs, which had their own wings and gave off intermittent buzzing sounds. Blanche Patch (39) recounts how one of these bombs landed close enough to Shaw's Corner to blow in one of his bedroom windows. "The glass flew clear of his bed, to which, finding that the rest of the household were safe, he retired unruffled."

97 The de Havilland Aircraft Company was a major manufacturer of fighter aircraft and bombers during World War II. Its head office was in Hatfield, about 8 km from Ayot St Lawrence.

98   The Women's Land Army was a civilian organization that arranged agricultural training and work for women during World War II.
99   Many goods, foods, and drinks (including tea) were rationed in Great Britain during World War II. All civilians, including children, were issued with ration books, which restricted what amounts they could buy.
100 Jisbella was a member of the Voluntary Aid Detachment, trained to provide nursing assistance to military personnel.
101 The Home Guard consisted of volunteers considered too old or medically unfit to serve in the armed forces.
102 Gabriel Pascal (1894–1954) was a Hungarian-born film producer who made films of four Shaw plays: *Pygmalion* (1938), for which Shaw won an Oscar (for the screenplay), *Major Barbara* (1941), *Caesar and Cleopatra* (1945), and *Androcles and the Lion* (1953). Of these, Jisbella seems only to have seen *Caesar and Cleopatra*, which she did not care for (*Postmistress*, p. 75). She also saw the film version of *The Doctor's Dilemma* (1958), produced by Anatole de Grunwald. She doesn't say if she enjoyed it, but she seems to have mistaken Leslie Caron for Vivien Leigh (*Postmistress*, p. 75). Shaw's relationship with Pascal is comprehensively documented in *Selected Correspondence of Bernard Shaw: Bernard Shaw and Gabriel Pascal*, ed. Bernard F. Dukore (Toronto: University of Toronto Press, 1996).
103 Esmé Percy (1887–1957) played several major Shaw roles, and appeared as Count Karpathy in the film version of *Pygmalion*. He was President of the Shaw Society from 1949 to 1957.
104 Shaw was one of numerous famous people photographed by Canadian Yousuf Karsh (1908–2002).
105 World War II ended with the surrender of Japan on 14 August 1945, though the celebrations described by Jisbella were on the occasion of the surrender of Germany on 7 May 1945.
106 Alice Laden (1901–79) served as Shaw's cook and housekeeper for the final few years of his life (after the death of Charlotte in 1943). Her *George Bernard Shaw Vegetarian Cookbook* was published in 1972. She was appointed the first Custodian of Shaw's Corner by the National Trust. Her recollections of Shaw ("I looked after Mr Shaw as I would a piece of rare Dresden China") are in Chappelow 25–36.
107 Launched in 1939, the battleship *Prince of Wales* was sunk by Japanese aircraft in December 1941 in the South China Sea with the loss of 327 lives.
108 See note 83.
109 Luton, a major transportation and industrial hub in Bedfordshire, is about 20 km northeast of Welwyn.
110 Clara Higgs was housekeeper at Shaw's Corner for forty-two years (1901–43). Her husband Harry was Shaw's head gardener during the same period. His

recollections of Shaw are in Chappelow 56–79. On Clara's death in 1948 Shaw paid for a handsome monument for her (and Harry) in Windelsham Cemetery (in Surrey).

111 Charlotte Shaw died on 12 September 1943. She and Shaw had been married for forty-five years.
112 Shaw's four-hundred-page political science manual was published in September 1944.
113 Echoing Eliza's "I'm a good girl, I am" in Act Two of *Pygmalion*.
114 Shaw's novella *The Adventures of the Black Girl in Her Search for God* was published by Constable in 1932.
115 *The Complete Plays of Bernard Shaw* was published (in one volume, with thirty-nine plays) by Constable in 1931.
116 For Jisbella's error about Vivien Leigh, see note 102.
117 While a notch below the crossword sophistication of *The Times*, the *Telegraph*'s crossword was not for cruciverbalist dilettantes.
118 A voluntary organization, established in Canada in 1897, that provides education and skills training for women. A newspaper report on Shaw's talk on Quarrelling is in Chappelow 98–100.
119 John Hunt is identified as an organ player in Chappelow 111. No information has come to light on his poet mother or on Beryl Ireland, but the photograph that Jisbella describes is reproduced in F.E. Loewenstein's *Bernard Shaw through the Camera* (London: B & H White, 1948) 42. The Rector is identified as the Reverend A.C.V. de Candole.
120 The ceremony took place on 10 April 1948. Shaw's speech is in Chappelow 267–68.
121 Clare (1894-1989) and Stephen (1893–1991) Winsten moved to Ayot in 1945. Clare's statue of Joan of Arc was installed in Shaw's garden in 1947. Stephen published four books on Shaw, all, says Shaw scholar and biographer Anthony Gibbs, "compromised by plagiarism, errors and deliberate misinformation" (*Chronology* 392).
122 The photograph has not been traced. There are no photographs of Jisbella in the extensive collection of photographs of and by Shaw held at the London School of Economics and Political Science.
123 Vassar College, in Poughkeepsie, NY, was founded as a private women's college in 1861. Like many US colleges and universities, then and now, Vassar frequently mounted productions of Shaw's plays.
124 The food parcel was sent by Isobel Joy Martin, a student at Vassar. She wrote to Jisbella on 1 November 1950 to let her know that the parcel was on its way: "I meant to send you one before, and to write to you, but I was busy with examinations and graduating from college." Ms Martin's *Life* article has not been traced. Her letter to Jisbella is in the Jisbella Lyth Collection.

125 Shaw was made a Freeman of the City of Dublin in February 1946 (Gibbs 327). In July 1936 Shaw and Charlotte—both born British subjects prior to Irish independence—registered as citizens of the Irish Free State but retained their British citizenship (Gibbs 303).

126 The "little guide" would become *Bernard Shaw's Rhyming Picture Guide to Ayot St Lawrence*, Shaw's last completed book, published on 14 December 1950, six weeks after his death, by the Leagrave Press in Luton. There was a simple paper-wrapped edition, and a more elegant hard cover edition. The paper edition sold for one shilling, the hard cover for five shillings.

127 Shaw was a lifelong anti-vivisectionist; he wrote and spoke about the subject frequently.

128 Sir Robert Ho Tung (1862–1956) was a wealthy Hong Kong businessman and philanthropist. Shaw met him in Hong Kong in February 1933. According to Blanche Patch (95), at Shaw's Corner Ho Tung and Shaw discussed "the Chinese scene" (Act Three) in *Buoyant Billions*, and—according to Holroyd (4:496)—Shaw also "conducted a miniature rehearsal" of the play in his garden (presumably on the occasion of Ho Tung's visit, though Holroyd isn't precise on this). Shaw's relationship with Ho Tung is discussed, *passim*, in Kay Li, *Bernard Shaw's Bridges to Chinese Culture* (Cham, Switzerland: Springer Nature for Palgrave Macmillan, 2016).

129 Danny Kaye (1913–87) was an American comedian and stage and film actor. According to Holroyd (4:496), Shaw "performed a garden pantomime" with Kaye.

130 The London Palladium variety theatre opened on Boxing Day 1910.

131 A swelling of the neck caused by an enlarged thyroid gland.

132 Robert Carleton Smith (1908–84) was music editor of *Esquire* magazine, and taught music history in American and British universities.

133 The gripping saga of the knockover jug that was an inkwell, not a jug, begins with Ellen Pollock's unappreciated gift to Shaw. As a vegetarian and anti-vivisectionist he was no doubt offended by a dead bison's foot, whatever its intended use. Why as a teetotaller it upset him it is difficult to know, unless the foot were big enough to serve as a beer jug—in which case it would have held enough ink to last a month of Sundays. Ellen Pollock (1902–97) was one of Shaw's favourite actresses. She acted in and directed many of his plays, in London, the provinces, and abroad. She was President of the Shaw Society from 1957 until her death. Mrs Thompson, one of Jisbella's neighbours, told Allan Chappelow (105) that she had purchased the inkwell after Shaw had disposed of it at the village fête—and proudly showed it to Chappelow (together with Shaw's inscription) when he interviewed her for his book. It is not clear how it later got back to another fête and, this time, failed to find a buyer until the enthusiastic Bermudan playwright came on the Jisbella scene and whisked it off across the ocean.

134 A town about 12 km north-east of Ayot St Lawrence.
135 "Eye-Witness" was a weekly current affairs programme broadcast on BBC Radio's Home Service every Wednesday at 1:10 pm.
136 Payment by instalments; a more formal term than "never-ever" (see note 59).
137 Though accounts of Shaw's accident vary considerably, his head gardener, Fred Drury, says it occurred while Shaw was pruning a greengage tree in his garden (Chappelow 52).
138 See note 126.
139 Shaw died of kidney failure at 4:59 a.m. on 2 November 1950.
140 Shaw was cremated at Golders Green Cemetery in North London on 6 November 1950, where Charlotte had been cremated on 15 September 1943. Charlotte's ashes were kept there until Shaw's death, after which they were mixed and scattered in the garden of Shaw's Corner on 23 November 1950.
141 The *Portsmouth Evening News* carried a short report on 6 November 1950 that Jisbella closed the post office for thirty minutes at the time of Shaw's cremation.
142 The National Trust became owner of Shaw's Corner (nationaltrust.org.uk/shaws-corner) in January 1944. Jisbella is correct in saying that Shaw gave no money for its upkeep.
143 "Thanks for Your Shilling," *Time* 61 (25 December 1950): 20, 23.
144 Actor-manager Richard Mansfield (1857–1907) directed and appeared (as Bluntschli) in *Arms and the Man*, the first Shaw play to be produced in America (the Herald Square Theatre, New York, 17 September 1894). Several Shaw plays had their world professional premières in America, including *The Devil's Disciple, Caesar and Cleopatra, Heartbreak House, Back to Methuselah, Saint Joan*, and *Village Wooing*. In *Caesar and Cleopatra* (New Amsterdam Theatre, New York, 30 October 1906) Johnston Forbes-Robertson (1853–1937) played opposite his wife, Gertrude Elliott (1874–1950). Archibald Henderson (1887–1963) was an American mathematics professor who became a friend and biographer of Shaw. His *magnum opus* on Shaw, incorporating material from previous books, was *George Bernard Shaw: Man of the Century* (New York: Appleton-Century-Crofts, 1956). Henderson's recollections of Shaw are in Chappelow 320–33.
145 Shaw's speech, which lasted an hour and forty minutes, was on 11 April 1933 to an audience of some 3,500. His topic, "The Future of Political Science in America," was a sustained, vigorous, and compelling attack on American capitalism.
146 Henry George (1839–97) was an American anarchist. His *Progress and Poverty* was published in 1879. Shaw heard him lecture in London on 5 September 1882.
147 On the contrary—Shaw, who visited Russia in 1931, expressed very positive views of Communism in his speech (published by Constable in August 1933).
148 It is not clear what fund the writer is referring to.

149 The 14 May 1951 issue of *Life* (pp 20–22) carried a brief illustrated article on the *Rhyming Guide* and a photograph of Jisbella in her post office. There was also a report of "angry" villagers at a protest meeting about tourists: close Shaw's Corner or provide adequate parking facilities, they demanded—or, some suggested, sell Shaw's Corner to America, and "let them take it down brick by brick and carry it across the ocean." There was extensive coverage of the dispute in the local and national press; several clippings are in the Jisbella Lyth Collection. "CHAOS IN MR SHAW'S VILLAGE" was a headline on the front page of the *Daily Mail* on 2 April 1951. As Jisbella and others predicted, the problems diminished as interest in Shaw faded.

150 Novelist and essayist G.K. Chesterton (1874-1936). A devout Catholic, Chesterton had several public debates with the sceptical Shaw on religious and social issues.

151 Shaw visited Yugoslavia in May 1929. The writer's "recollections" have not been traced.

152 The "Ayot St Lawrence Edition" of *The Collected Works of Bernard Shaw* (30 volumes) was published between 1930 and 1932 in New York by Wm H. Wise & Company.

153 Catherine Parr, Henry VIII's sixth and last wife, married Thomas Seymour soon after Henry's death in 1547. She died in childbirth in 1548. It is not clear what "direct lineal descendant" Jisbella's correspondent had in mind, or what the Ayot connection is.

154 I.e., to the Brocket Arms.

155 To be dressed in one's bib and tucker is to be wearing one's best clothes.

156 Although Dame Edith Evans's (1888–1976) most famous role was Lady Bracknell in Oscar Wilde's *The Importance of Being Earnest*, she acted frequently in Shaw plays (at Malvern, for example, in *The Apple Cart* and *Heartbreak House*).

157 The Automobile Association, a motoring club founded in 1905.

158 Hampstead Heath is a large open park (about eight-hundred acres) located 6 km north of the centre of London.

159 The *Daily Herald* (2 April 1951) dubbed the conflict between villagers and visitors "The Battle of Shaw's Corner." "Angry villagers," the *Herald* reported, "glowered as cars, buses, and cycles churned up their lanes and made 'porridge' of their paths."

160 Stratford-upon-Avon, Shakespeare's birthplace, and home to the Royal Shakespeare Company, has long been a heavily commercialized magnet for tourists.

161 The Transatlantic Quiz was a weekly general knowledge competition between British and American teams, broadcast by the BBC and NBC. The British quiz master at the time that Jisbella was listening was Alistair Cooke (1908–2004); the American quiz master was Lionel Hale (1909–77).

162 On p. 33 of *Thirty Years with G.B.S.*
163 Christopher Morley (1890–1957) was an American writer and stage director. His joke—with racist overtones—presumably links the name Jisbella with the Biblical Jezebel, the stereotype of female sensuousness and promiscuity to be found, Morley believes, among dark-skinned women in iniquitous locales such as Havana.
164 In June 1951. Brenda Bruce (1919–96) played opposite Maurice Denham (1909–2002).
165 Gin and Italian (= "it") sweet vermouth.
166 A popular BBC radio comedy and entertainment show.
167 At the Royal Court Theatre, July 1952. Ellen Pollock (who also directed) played opposite Michael Golden (1913–83). The playbill also included a new play by H.F. Rubinstein called *Bernard Shaw in Heaven*, which, *The Times* reported (28 July 1952), "makes rather heavy weather of the great man's arrival in the outer courts."
168 Tallulah Bankhead (1903–68) was an American stage and film actress, with a distinctive (husky) voice.
169 There are 14 lbs to a stone.
170 A boat race between Oxford and Cambridge universities, first held in 1829. It has been an annual event on the River Thames since 1856, and still attracts wide public interest.
171 King Michael I (1921–2017) was the last king of Romania. He was forced to abdicate in December 1947 by Romania's communist government. Ex-king Michael and his family moved to Ayot in July 1952 and lived there until September 1954, when they moved to Switzerland (Porter 212–13, 218).
172 Prince Charles (born 1948) is the eldest child of Queen Elizabeth II (born 1926, acceded to the throne 1952) and heir apparent to the throne of the United Kingdom. Princess Anne (born 1950) is the Queen's second child.
173 Carola Oman, Lady Lenanton (1897–1978) was a novelist, biographer, and historian. She died in Ayot St Lawrence. There is a memorial to her and her husband in the village church.
174 Fred Boucher and his wife became custodians of Shaw's Corner in 1952. Alice Laden retired after growing depressed over "all those strangers walking about the house and all over the garden, and dropping their tickets on the ground and dirtying the place with their muddy boots. I think that would have horrified Mr Shaw" (Chappelow 36).
175 From Thomas Gray's "Elegy Written in a Country Churchyard" (1751).
176 Evelyn Newman (1920–2015) was an American businesswoman and philanthropist who won numerous awards for her support of education and the arts. She was married to a leading numismatist, Eric Newman, not to the President of the United States.

177 In addition to the door-knocker, Rosalind Danecourt (sometimes known as Rosie Banks Danecourt) created four plaster plaques of Shaw and a brass relief portrait, all held at Shaw's Corner.

178 Playwright and critic St John Ervine (1883–1971) published his biography of Shaw, *Bernard Shaw: His Life, Work and Friends*, in 1956.

179 Queen Victoria is said to have responded "We are not amused" to a risqué story at a dinner party.

180 The young woman was Romie Lambkin (see Introduction pp. 4–5). She needed shilling coins to feed the meter in her home to maintain the electricity supply.

181 Torca Cottage, where Shaw and his family lived for several months in 1886, and visited frequently for some years, is in Dalkey, a small coastal town a few kilometres south of Dublin.

182 I.e., Blaise (Bullimore). See Acknowledgments p. ix and Preface p. 10.

183 An advertisement in the *Manchester Guardian* on 4 March 1954 indicated that the rent for Shaw's Corner was £175 a year: "In addition, the tenant would have to pay all outgoings, including rates of £92 a year, and would be responsible for interior repairs, decoration, outside painting, and the upkeep of the grounds. He [sic] would be required to show the study and gardens to the public on behalf of the National Trust on Saturdays and would have to keep as they are the study and garden hut where Shaw did much of his work."

184 Public relations executive Christopher Casserley and his family (mother, wife, and two children) took up the tenancy in August 1956 (*Londonderry Sentinel*, 28 July 1956).

185 Jisbella's exhausting tour of Venice took in the main tourist sights, including explorer Marco Polo's (1254–1324) home on the Calle Scaleta, near the Rialto; the Salute Church where Italian socialite Princess Ira von Fürstenberg (b. 1940) was married as a teenage bride (in 1955); and the Bridge of Sighs, which connects the interrogation rooms in the Doge's Palace to the palace prisons. (Prisoners could take one last glance at the Venice lagoon through a small barred window on the bridge, and sigh as they were led to the cells.)

186 Zoe Dyke (1896–1975) operated a large silk farm (now closed) at Lullingstone Castle in Kent. The Ayot St Lawrence location was established in December 1956 (reported in *The Times*, 5 December 1956) and was short-lived.

187 A BBC Radio programme advertised as being about "interesting people who are In Town [London] Tonight," broadcast in the BBC Home Service on Saturdays at 7:30 pm.

188 Jill Adams (1930–2008) was a stage and film actress. She married Peter Haigh (1925–2001), a BBC television announcer, in 1957.

189 See note 103.

SOURCES CITED

Chappelow, Allan. *Shaw the Villager and Human Being. A Biographical Symposium.* London: Charles Skilton, 1961.
Gibbs, A.M. *A Bernard Shaw Chronology.* Houndmills, Basingstoke: Palgrave, 2001.
Holroyd, Michael. *Bernard Shaw.* 5 vols. London: Chatto & Windus, 1988–92.
Patch, Blanche. *Thirty Years with G.B.S.* London: Gollancz, 1951.
Porter, Ivor. *Michael of Romania: the King and the Country.* Stroud: Sutton, 2005.
Shaw, Bernard. *Bernard Shaw's Rhyming Picture Guide to Ayot Saint Lawrence.* Luton: Leagrave Press, 1950.

OTHER SOURCES CONSULTED
British Newspaper Archive: https://www.britishnewspaperarchive.co.uk.
Laurence, Dan H., ed. *Bernard Shaw: A Bibliography.* 2 vols. Oxford: Clarendon Press, 1983.
——. *Bernard Shaw: Collected Letters.* 4 vols. New York: Viking Penguin, 1985–88.
Loewenstein, F.L. *Bernard Shaw through the Camera.* London: B & H White, 1948.
Mander, Raymond, and Joe Mitchenson. *Theatrical Companion to Shaw.* New York: Pitman, 1955.
Newspapers.com: https://www.newspapers.com.
Rumball, Louise. *George Bernard Shaw and Ayot St Lawrence. Memories and Facts by a Villager 1905–1930.* Harpenden, Hertfordshire: SDS MediaPrint, 1987.
The Times Digital Archive: https://www.gale.com/c/the-times-digital-archive.
Wearing, J.P. *American and British Theatrical Biography: A Directory.* Metuchen, NJ: Scarecrow Press, 1979.

INDEX

"Abide with Me" (hymn) 32
Adams, Jill 120
Adventures of the Black Girl in Her Search for God, The (Shaw) 75
Alhambra Theatre, Seattle 122n19
American Society of Political Science 94
Ames, Captain L.G. 50
Androcles and the Lion (Shaw) 2
Anne, Princess 111
Anne, Queen (of Romania) 111, 116-17
Apple Cart, The (Shaw) 2
Arms and the Man (Shaw) 94
Arts Theatre, London 108
Ash, Surrey 22
Astor Hotel, Hong Kong 38
Ayot St Lawrence, Hertfordshire, England 1, 2, 7-11, 41, 46, 47
    Ayot House 46, 70, 78, 117, 119
    Brocket Arms 5, 49, 125n69
    Brocket Hall 125n63
    New Church 48, 49, 76, 78
    New Rectory 49
    Old Church 48, 49, 77, 106, 117
    Old Rectory 49
    Three Horseshoes 124n69
    The village is connected to electricity supply 69
    In World War II 70-72
    Tourists after Shaw's death 105
    Villagers' anger at tourists 106-107
    See also Shaw's Corner
Ayot St Peter, Hertfordshire, England 49

Back to Methuselah (Shaw) 2
Bankhead, Tallulah 109
Bay of Biscay 23, 40
Bernard Shaw's Rhyming Picture Guide to Ayot Saint Lawrence 3-4, 78-79, 89, 91, 92, 93, 106, 112
Bison's foot, the curious story of 130n133
Boer War 22
Boleyn, Anne 49-50
Boucher, Mr & Mrs Fred 112, 117
Bournemouth, Hampshire 40
Bradford, Yorkshire 44
Brighton, Sussex 41
British Broadcasting Corporation (BBC) 86-87, 91-92, 107-108, 115, 119
Brockenhurst, Hampshire 16, 23, 82-83
Brocket, Lord and Lady (*see also* Nall-Cain) 57
Brown, Mason 107
Bruce, Brenda 108
Bullimore, Blaise 8-11, 14
Buoyant Billions (Shaw) 130n128

Caesar and Cleopatra (Shaw) 75, 94
Candida (Shaw) 1
Carl Rosa Opera Company 21
Caron, Leslie 128n102
Caruso, Enrico 29
Casserley, Christopher, and family 117, 118
Chappelow, Allan 3, 4, 121n1
Charles, Prince of Wales 111
Chautauqua Building, New York 28
Chesterton, G.K. 96
Chicago, Illinois 28
Churchill, Winston 103, 112, 113
Colombo, Sri Lanka 23, 39
Columbia Broadcasting System (CBS) 87
Common Sense About the War (Shaw) 2
Complete Plays of Bernard Shaw 75
Coney Island, New York 31
Cooke, Alistair 132n161
Cooper, Gladys 65
Currall, Ivo L. 64, 65, 72, 73, 74, 89

Daily Telegraph, The 76
Dalkey, Ireland 134n181
Danecourt, Rosalind 112
Daughter of the Gods, The (silent movie) 29
Day, Fred 55, 77, 89, 90
De Candole, A.C.V. 129n119
De Grunwald, Anatole 128n102
De Havilland Aircraft Company 70
Denham, Maurice 108
Devil's Disciple, The (Shaw) 131n144
Diocesan Boys' School, Hong Kong 35
Doctor's Dilemma, The (Shaw) 1, 75
Drury, Fred 131n137
Dyke, Zoe, Lady Hart Dyke 119-20

Earl's Court, London 20
Echo of Seals, An (Lambkin) 4
Ediss, Connie 54, 55
Elegy Written in a Country Churchyard (Gray) 112

Elizabeth II, Queen 111
Elliott, Gertrude 94
Empress of Asia 25
Ervine, St John 113
Evans, Edith, Dame 106
Everybody's Political What's What? (Shaw) 2, 94
"Eye-Witness" (BBC Radio programme) 86-87

Fairbanks, Douglas 29
Forbes-Robertson, Johnston 94
Fürstenberg, Princess Ira von 134n185

Galsworthy, John 67
George, Henry 94
German Evangelical Lutheran Church, Seattle 28
Gibbs, Anthony 129n121
Golden, Michael 133n167
Golders Green Crematorium 90
Goodman, Colonel T.C. 26, 27
Gray, Thomas 133n175
Gulf of Aden 124n51

Haigh, Peter 120
Haiphong, Vietnam 39
Hale, Lionel 107, 108
Harding family 125n69
Harpenden, Hertfordshire 51, 57
Harrogate, Yorkshire 43
Hartlepool, Yorkshire 44
Hatfield, Hertfordshire 70
Healey, Michael 121n1
Heartbreak House (Shaw) 2
Hell's Gate, British Columbia 123n37
Henderson, Archibald, 94
Henry VIII, King 49-50, 102
Hertfordshire Mercury 68
Higgs, Clara 74
Higgs, Harry 128n110

Hippodrome, The, New York 29
HMS *The Prince of Wales* 72
Ho Tung, Sir Robert 80, 81
Holroyd, Michael 130n128, 130n129
Home Guard, The 71
Hong Kong 23, 24, 25, 33, 35-39, 41, 63, 67, 80
How to Settle the Irish Question (Shaw) 2
Hunt, John 76
Hunt, Phoebe 27
Hyderabad Bulletin 68

Importance of Being Earnest, The (Wilde) 132n156
"In Town Tonight" (BBC Radio programme) 119
Intelligent Woman's Guide to Socialism, The (Shaw) 2, 94
Inwood, Henry 125n64
Inwood, William 125n64
Ireland, Beryl 76
Irish Times 4
Iroquois Hotel, New York 28

Jackson, Sir Barry 127n92
Japanese Whispers (Lambkin) 4
Jefferson, Thomas 123n34
"Jesus Shall Reign Where'er the Sun" (hymn) 33
John Bull's Other Island (Shaw) 1

Karsh, Yousuf (of Ottawa) 72
Kaye, Danny 81
Kellermann, Annette 29
Kimpton, Hertfordshire 73, 74
Kingsley School for Boys, Essex Fells, New Jersey 29
Kuala Lumpur, Malaysia 24

Laden, Alice 72, 75, 76, 90, 92, 108, 112
Lambkin, Romie 4-5, 13, 14, 117
Land Army Girls 70

Lawrence, Thomas Edward (Lawrence of Arabia) 57
Le Havre, France 40
Leagrave Press 89, 92
Leeds, Yorkshire 43
Leigh, Vivien 75
Life magazine 9, 78, 95, 97
Little Man, The (Galsworthy) 67
Little Theatre, London 65, 66
Loewenstein, Fritz Erwin 64, 72, 73, 74
London Palladium 81
Lullingstone Castle Silk Farm 119
Luton, Bedfordshire 74
Lyceum Theatre, New York 29
Lyde, Sir Lionel and Lady 48-49
Lyte, Henry Francis 123n35
Lyth, Ambrose 25, 31, 32, 57
   Meets Jisbella 21
   Early career 21-22
   Army service in South Africa 22
   Marries Jisbella 22
   Army service in Hong Kong 24, 35-40
   Witnesses deadly fire in Hong Kong 37-38
   Celebrates end of World War I 38
   Awarded Meritorious Medal for war service 39
   Returns to England 41
   Leaves the Army 42
   Unemployed 43
   Illnesses 41, 45
   Sundry jobs in Yorkshire 43-45
   Appointed postmaster at Ayot St Lawrence 47
   Meets Shaw 48
   Death and funeral 50-51
Lyth, Jisbella 3-4, 5, 7-12, 13, 14
   Childhood 15-17
   Early jobs 19-21
   Courtship and marriage 21-22
   Honeymoon 22
   Travels to Hong Kong 23

Travels to North America 25-26
In Vancouver 25
In Seattle 25-28
In Chicago 28
In New York 28-32
Ill health 30-31, 57, 81-82, 83, 89, 109-111, 113, 118
Returns to Hong Kong 33
In Yokohama 33
Teaches in Hong Kong 33-37
Experiences earthquake in Hong Kong 38
Celebrates the end of World War I 38
Travels to England 39
First sees Shaw 40
Sundry jobs in Yorkshire 43-45
Converts to Catholicism 44
Re-marries Ambrose in Catholic Church 44
Jobs in Hertfordshire 45-46
Appointed postmistress at Ayot St Lawrence 50
First impressions of Shaw 53
Sells Shaw's photographs and letters 54-56
Hard time understanding Shaw's works 57, 75
But enjoys reading *Pygmalion* 75
Press reports her "fondling" Shaw's photographs 57-58
Newspaper pays damages for the "fondling" story 60
"The Lady with Three Dogs" 60
Opens a tea room and garden 61
Model for "Z" in *Village Wooing* 65-68
Sees *Village Wooing* 67
Called "the most remarkable character in the village next to Shaw" 69
Takes in war evacuees 70
Receives American food parcels 71
Trains for the Voluntary Aid Detachment 71

Supports village charity events during the war 71
Celebrates the end of war in Europe 72
Hears news of Charlotte Shaw's death 74
Sees films of Shaw's plays 75
Shaw helps Jisbella with the *Daily Telegraph* crossword puzzle 76
Discusses with Shaw the selling price of his *Rhyming Picture Guide* 78-79
Responds to press enquiries about Shaw 80
Visits her birthplace (Brockenhurst, Hampshire) 82-83
Appears (with Shaw) in a newsreel for Shaw's 94th birthday 85-86
Interviewed by the BBC 86-87
Interviewed by the Columbia Broadcasting System 87
Last conversation with Shaw 87
Sells more Shaw letters 88
Anxiety over Shaw's health 88-89
Reaction to Shaw's death 90
Her living room is a "shrine" 91
Appears on BBC television 91-92
Dispute with Leagrave Press over selling rights for the *Rhyming Picture Guide* 92
Mails copies of the *Rhyming Picture Guide* around the world 93-103
Income from the *Rhyming Picture Guide* 103
Salvages books from Shaw's Corner 105
Attends opening of Shaw's Corner 105
On the tourist invasion of Ayot St Lawrence 106-108
On the pronunciation of her surname 107-108
Sees London revivals of *Village Wooing* 108-109
Celebrates her birthday in hospital 110
Meets ex-King of Romania and his family 111

Declines invitation to visit America 113
Escapes fire at the post office 115
Interviewed by the BBC for the BBC Italian Service 115
European travels: Switzerland, Austria, Germany, Lichtenstein, Italy 115-16, 118

Macau Island, Hong Kong 39
Major Barbara (Shaw) 1, 94
Malvern, Worcestershire 68
Malvern Festival 127n92
Man and Superman (Shaw) 1, 94
Manila, Philippines 25
Mansfield, Richard 94, 131n144
Maresfield, Sussex 41
Marseilles, France 40
Martin, Joy 129n124
Metropolitan Opera House, New York 94
Michael I, King (of Romania) 111, 116-17
Millionairess, The (Shaw) 2
Misalliance (Shaw) 2
Monte Carlo 11
Montreal, Quebec 32
Moose Jaw, Saskatchewan 32
Morley, Christopher 107
Mount Etna, Sicily 40
Mrs Warren's Profession (Shaw) 94
"Much-Binding-in-the-Marsh" (BBC Radio programme) 108
My Time in The War (Lambkin) 4

Nall-Cain, Charles (Lord Brocket) 46, 50
National Broadcasting Company (NBC) 132n161
National Health Service 65
National Trust 1, 7, 91, 105, 112, 117
New Washington Hotel, Seattle 26
New York 28-32
New York Theatre Guild 94
New York Times 69, 94
Newman, Eric 133n176

Newman, Evelyn 112
Niven, Paul 87

"Old Folks' Longing, The" 121n4
Oman, Carola, Lady Lenanton 111-12, 126n78
On the Rocks (Shaw) 2, 127n87
Orme, Ted 64, 65
Orpheum Theatre, Seattle 27

Parr, Catherine 102
Pascal, Gabriel 72, 94
Patch, Blanche 55, 67, 75, 107, 120
Pavlova, Anna 29
Pelham, New York 31
Penang, Malaysia 24
Percy, Esmé 72, 120
Pickford, Mary 29
Political Madhouse in America and Nearer Home, The (Shaw) 2
Pollock, Ellen 82, 109
Presley, Elvis 122n17
Princes Risborough, Buckinghamshire 22
Progress and Poverty (George) 94
Proud (Healey) 121n1
Pygmalion (Shaw) 2, 75, 94

Red Sea 124n51
Revett, Nicholas 49
Rice, Captain Emery 29
Roosevelt Hospital, New York 31
Roosevelt, Eleanor 112
Roosevelt, James Henry 123n31
Royal Court Theatre, London 1, 109
Rubinstein, H.F. 133n167

Saigon, Vietnam 39
SS *Borneo* 23
SS *Mongolia* 123n28
SS *Monteagle* 33
SS *Sphinx* 39

St George's Church, Montreal 32
Saint Joan (Shaw) 2, 4, 94
St Pancras Church, London 49
Sea of Japan 25
Seattle, Washington 26-28
Selsey, Valentine 87, 90
Seymour, Thomas 132n153
Shaw, Bernard 1-5, 8-9, 40-41, 47, 48, 50
   Offers condolences on the death of Ambrose 51
   Offers photographs to Jisbella for sale in the post office 54
   Generous to villagers 56
   Experiences bombing damage to Shaw's Corner 70
   Photographed by Karsh 72
   Gives Jisbella copies of his work 75
   Gives talk to the Ayot Women's Institute 76
   Attends meeting of village boys' club 76
   Attends Ayot organ recital 76
   Attends and speaks at dedication of new gates for the Ayot Old Church 77
   His 90th birthday 77
   Made Freeman of the City of Dublin 78
   Proposes writing *Bernard Shaw's Rhyming Picture Guide to Ayot Saint Lawrence* 78
   Puts his car and chauffeur at Jisbella's disposal for hospital travel 81
   His 94th birthday 83
   Falls in his garden 88
   Returns to Shaw's Corner after hospitalization 89
   Death 90
   Cremation 90
   Ashes scattered at Shaw's Corner 2, 90
   See also titles of individual works
Shaw, Charlotte 1, 9, 51, 58, 74
Shaw in Heaven (Rubinstein) 109
Shaw Society, UK 73, 120

Shaw's Corner
   Named by Shaw 54-55
   Given to the National Trust 91
   Official opening 105-106
   Tenants 112, 117
   Re-opening 119-20
Singapore 24
Smith, Robert Carleton 82
South, Mary Ann 126n79
Southampton, Hampshire 40, 71
Stevenage, Hertfordshire 86
Strait of Gibraltar 122n13
Strait of Messina, Italy 40
Stratford-upon-Avon, Warwickshire
Suez Canal 39
Swatow (Hong Kong) earthquake 38

Tatler, The 69
Tel Aviv, Israel 93
Tetrazzini, Luisa 29
Thorndike, Sibyl 65, 66, 67
Three Horseshoes, The 125n69
Time magazine 9, 93, 95, 97, 102
Too True to be Good (Shaw) 127n87
"Trans Atlantic Quiz" (UK-USA radio programme) 107
Tuke, A.W. 125n67
20,000 Leagues Under the Sea (movie) 29

Vancouver, British Columbia 32-33
Vancouver Club 32
Vancouver Hotel 32
Vassar College, Poughkeepsie, New York 78
Village Wooing (Shaw) 2, 3, 65-68, 75, 108, 109, 112
Vincent, Henri 123n29
Voluntary Aid Detachment 71

Walker, William Bradley and family 25-33
Washington, George 31
Watts, Isaac 124n41

Weintraub, Stanley 126n80
Welwyn Garden City, Hertfordshire 45, 74
West Hartlepool, Yorkshire 71
West Point 31
Wheathampstead, Hertfordshire 40, 45
Wheatleigh, Edward 127n88
Whitby, Yorkshire 43
White, Harold 92
White Plains, New York 31
Wilde, Oscar 132n156
Wilkes Stock Company, Seattle 27

Willard Parker Hospital, New York 30, 31
Winsten, Clare 77
Winsten, Stephen 129n121
Women's Institute, The 76
Women's Land Army, The 70
Wontner, Arthur 65, 66, 67
"Write Them a Letter Tonight" 121n4

Yokohama, Japan 25, 33
YWCA, Vancouver 33

www.ingramcontent.com/pod-product-compliance
Lightning Source LLC
Chambersburg PA
CBHW030909080526
44589CB00010B/225